ANGER
Deal With It, Heal With It, Stop It From Killing You

Bill DeFoore, Ph.D.

Health Communications, Inc.
Deerfield Beach, Florida

Bill DeFoore
Irving, Texas

Library of Congress Cataloging-in-Publication Data
DeFoore, Bill
    Anger: deal with it, heal with it, stop it from killing you / Bill
DeFoore.
    p.   cm.
    ISBN 1-55874-162-3
    1. Anger. I. Title.
BF575.A5D64   1991   91-8033
152.4′7—dc20   CIP

© 1991 Bill DeFoore
ISBN 1-55874-162-3

Publisher: Health Communications, Inc.
              3201 S.W. 15th Street
              Deerfield Beach, Florida 33442-8190

DEDICATION

To Donna LeBlanc for her
friendship and her inspiration
in getting this work into print.

To my parents, John and Telle DeFoore,
for their love and encouragement.

CONTENTS

INTRODUCTION

Sam had a look of indignant rage in his eyes. The lines of his face curved and formed outlines of his anger, which seemed to flow from his eyes in streams. He was hard to look at. I felt as if I had done something wrong, even though I had only known the man for a few moments. It would have been easy to feel afraid or guilty, looking into those accusing eyes.

When he spoke, I was amazed to hear his mild tone and pleasant voice. It was as if the eyes had been lying. His words told the story of a passive man, afraid of his 22-year-old son, afraid of his wife and afraid of facing what he had done to create the misery in his family. Sam's words told me nothing of the anger in his eyes.

Oh, he was at war, all right — with himself. "At times," he said, "my chest burns as if there is a red-hot iron piercing my heart." Sam was all too well armed with guilt and anger at himself, and his body was the battleground.

In the battle with his wife and son, however, he was unarmed. He was a helpless victim. At least, that's how it seemed to him.

Sam hated his anger. But he couldn't make it go away. It just got stronger and more disturbing. It turned into rage. As a matter of fact, the rage that was growing in his family was destroying his home.

I hope reading this book will help you learn to make a
friend of your anger and express it in healthy ways. Like
Sam, you have probably figured out that you can't make it
go away, no matter how hard you try.

THE PRESSURE COOKER

Most of us find ourselves exploding from time to time
and regretting it later. The explosions occur because we
don't like our anger and we try to keep it inside. It works
like a pressure cooker. We can only suppress or apply
pressure against our anger for so long before it erupts.
Periodic eruptions can cause all kinds of problems.

At Sam's house, the pressure cooker was about to blow.
No one had "let the steam out" in a long time. The last
pressure release had been six months ago when Sam's
son, Joe, had taken a neighbor's car and run it off a bridge.
Joe wasn't hurt but the car was a total loss. Of course,
Joe's parents paid for it. And paid for it. And paid for it.
They always paid. But at least the pressure was off — for
a while.

It only took a few more months for Joe to reach a
boiling point again. He just wasn't as good as Mom and
Dad at stuffing feelings. It seemed to be his job in the
family to let the steam out of the family pressure cooker.
This time he really blew the top off.

Sam and his wife, Margaret, had been out of town
visiting relatives for the weekend. They had been very
nervous about leaving. As a matter of fact, this had been
their first trip together for pure pleasure in quite some
time. They were usually far too worried about Joe to
leave home for long. Their two daughters were grown,
and it seemed now that Joe was all they could think about.

As they were driving home, they were quiet. Each was
wondering what their son was going to do next. As they
turned down their street, they heard the sirens.

Without knowing why, Sam and Margaret looked at
each other and panic filled their eyes. They didn't say a
word. Then they saw their house in flames.

The fireman knew who they were by the looks on their faces. He walked up to them slowly and said, "Your son is over there. I'm afraid your home is a total loss. We got here too late. Your neighbor called and when we arrived, we found the house consumed in flames and your son sitting right there, acting as if nothing had happened."

They looked where he was pointing and saw Joe sitting on the ground, poking at something with a stick. The look on his face didn't make any sense. You would never have known from looking at him that his family's home was burning down just a few hundred feet away.

As they approached, they saw that what Joe was holding wasn't a stick. It was a large kitchen knife. On the ground in front of him was a family portrait, showing him and his mother with their arms around each other. His father was off to the side with his arms around his two daughters. Everyone in the picture was smiling except Joe. He was stabbing the family portrait while his house was burning. But he didn't feel any pressure. He had started the fire.

Maybe you believe you don't have any anger. You've succeeded in stuffing, controlling or stifling that "unpleasant" part of yourself. This would work fine if there weren't a fire under the pressure cooker. But there is.

Everything we are learning about emotions and health tells us it is unhealthy to stuff feelings. Your efforts to control your anger may be hurting you. If you don't blow, like an overheated pressure cooker, you may have an internal explosion. This usually means depression, self-hatred, major illness or all of the above.

Learning to express anger without there being a victim is the key to your empowerment. For healing and recovery or for making your dreams come true, the healthy release of your anger is part of the emotional empowerment you need to face and overcome the tremendous obstacles in your life.

WHO COULD POSSIBLY LIKE ANGER?

With all of the abuse and conflict in the world, it seems anger is the problem, not the solution. Victims of abuse, perpetrators of abuse and rescuers of abusers have problems with anger — their own and others. When it comes to abuse, it seems anger is the bad guy.

Anger is usually expressed in ways that make someone a victim. We often get anger mixed up with aggression and attack. Most people believe anger is just plain bad and the world would be a better place without it.

I had just been introduced to a crowd of about 100 people who had given up three hours of their Saturday morning to learn about "Anger Management And Healthy Emotional Expression." I asked, "Somebody give me a definition of anger." I love asking this question. Most people don't know what anger is. We think about it, talk about it, feel it and act on it. But we don't know what it is.

No one said anything for about a minute. I could almost see the cogs turning in their minds as they struggled to define something they thought they knew about. I smiled. "Isn't that interesting? It's not easy to define, is it? Just give me some words you associate with anger."

"Rage!" from a woman in back of the room. I could see it in her eyes.

"Hurting people," was offered by a small quiet man in the front row who had one of those strained but permanent smiles on his face.

"Losing control," was the definition proposed by a dignified man in a business suit who had bloodshot eyes. I could see how hard he had been fighting with himself to stay in control.

"How do you think the dictionary defines anger?" I challenged them one more time.

A bright, attractive woman offered, "It's an emotion."

"Bingo! That's it! It's just an emotion. It doesn't hurt anybody," I said, enjoying the looks on their faces as they heard this for the first time.

"There's one more part of the definition that is really important. The emotion of anger is for our protection." No one disagreed. They never do. It was as if they knew, but didn't know that they knew.

"Anger is just an emotion. Emotions are part of who we are, like our heads, hearts and hands. All emotions are okay. The dictionary definition of anger that I like best is, *'A feeling one has toward something that offends, opposes or annoys.'* There's nothing malicious or mean in the basic feeling of anger."

Anger is for our protection against something that hurts or threatens to hurt us. Where would we be without it? Maybe stuck on a mountainside in freezing temperatures in the middle of the night.

I'M TOO MAD TO DIE!

A friend of mine named Dayna was on a backpacking trip in the Rockies when she learned the value of her own anger. She and her friend Lynn had been traveling around in an old Volkswagen bug for several weeks when they decided to hike up into the mountains and do some camping. Neither of them had much experience in this, but they were adventurous and carefree — a combination which almost proved deadly.

Lynn had seemed to be the one who had it all together during the trip. She was bold in talking to strangers, getting free meals and finding places to stay. Dayna was more shy and reserved, holding back in many situations where Lynn seemed brave and daring. Lynn's bravado led to some pretty hairy situations, but nothing compared to their experience on the mountain.

It was Lynn's idea to keep hiking, even when it started getting cold and the sun was settling behind the nearby snow-capped peaks. Dayna protested, but as usual, Lynn insisted. Soon it became apparent that they were in trouble.

They came to a place on the mountain where they could not go any higher. There were no more trees to hold onto and the slopes were getting steeper. Both of them were amateur climbers at best. They were not equipped to spend the night on the mountain, even if there had been a place to put a bedroll.

Suddenly Dayna noticed a change in Lynn. She got quiet and started making little whimpering sounds. Her hands and legs were starting to tremble. When she looked into Lynn's eyes, Dayna could actually see her collapsing inside.

Lynn whispered in a small, weak voice, "Dayna, I have to tell you something. I have a fear of heights."

"Now she tells me," thought Dayna.

Just at that moment, the mountain seemed to push against Lynn's backpack and dislodge her sleeping bag. Before Dayna could reach it, it was tumbling down the mountain.

Unsteady on their feet, they watched in silence as the sleeping bag bounced all the way into the ravine that stretched into the blackness below them. There was a moment of silence that seemed to vibrate with their fear. They were suddenly aware that their lives were hanging by a thread. Little did they know the thread that would save them was Dayna's anger.

A light snow started to fall and the wind picked up a little, making a low moaning sound. There was a desolate, lonely feeling in the air. Lynn seemed to be fading into the side of the cliff. But not Dayna.

Dayna felt herself getting hot inside. At first she didn't know what it was. Then she suddenly realized. She was furious! Without knowing what she was saying or why, Dayna started screaming at Lynn, at God and at the mountain. She told all three of them that her time was not up!

"I'm not ready to die!" she screamed, "And I sure don't plan to end my life on this cold, lonely mountain or tumbling down the side of it! I've come too far and been through too much to quit now!"

She stood up, grabbed Lynn's pack and slung it over her shoulder with her own. In a voice she barely recognized as hers, she said to Lynn, "Get up! We're going down!"

Lynn was whining by now and not making much sense. She was terrified of the situation, but she was even more afraid of the rage in Dayna.

She was still talking about being afraid of heights when Dayna took her by the arm and pulled her up until they were face to face. Looking hard into Lynn's frightened eyes, Dayna said in a forceful and confident voice, "We are going down, because I'm taking us down. You are going to be just fine. Hold on to me and shut up."

Dayna had not felt so powerful since the time she beat up the neighborhood bully when she was eight years old. Anger had been her ally before and it came to her aid now. Her body felt strong and steady as she helped her trembling friend down the side of the mountain in the cold windy twilight. She did not really know what had happened and she didn't question it. Only years later did she realize that her anger had saved her life.

Although her life had been far from wonderful, Dayna was determined not to lose it. The result had been an empowering anger that allowed her to do exactly what needed to be done. Dayna discovered the survival value of her anger.

I DON'T WANT TO LOSE CONTROL

In my counseling practice, I do a lot of rage and anger work. I always encourage my clients to voice their fears about expressing their anger, and one of the most common statements I hear is, "I don't want to lose control."

When we are afraid of losing control, it's not anger we are afraid of. The wild, destructive force we sometimes feel inside is rage. *Rage is a mixture of unexpressed pain, fear and anger that has been building up over a long period of time.* It results from being hurt and scared and keeping all the feelings inside. If we return to our story about Sam and his family, maybe we can learn more about the results of suppressed rage and the fear of losing control.

In my counseling sessions with Sam, I made my best effort to ignore the look in his eyes and concentrate on his words. I didn't understand the story his eyes told. I thought I'd better listen and see how he explained what was going on behind those eyes.

I learned that Sam was the son of a chronic compulsive gambler and had grown up in a very mixed-up family. His mother was a rageaholic and the target for her rage was his father.

When his dad wasn't around, however, which was most of the time, Mom took her anger out on Sam. He was the victim of his mother's displaced anger. He had learned from a very early age to protect himself and keep peace in his family by being quiet and withdrawn and never, never showing his anger. He learned the importance of staying "in control."

Sam had continued to be passive and control his emotions throughout all of his adult life. This had been necessary in his childhood, but it just wasn't working anymore. In his current family something else was called for.

His son needed him to be strong and take charge of the family and Sam didn't know how to do it. Joe needed the security of knowing that his dad was in control. Without realizing it, Sam had suppressed his strength and power along with his anger. The rage Sam had seen and been hurt by in his past was a sick distortion of anger mixed with hurt and fear. When he suppressed his anger, he lost his ability to claim his strength against anything which threatened him or those he loved. There was no "tough" in his love.

In his mind Sam was powerless over the situation at home. As long as he hated and suppressed his anger, he indeed was powerless.

His son was not in control consciously, but he ruled the family. As a matter of fact, he lost control on a fairly regular basis. After the fire, Joe began exhibiting violent rage, with threats to hurt himself and his parents.

It seemed that Joe was expressing his father's rage along with his own. He was also abusing alcohol, which seemed to reliably trigger the rage attacks. This was beginning to occur all too frequently.

Sam's fear of losing control was causing him to do just that. By suppressing the anger and rage of a lifetime, he gave up his power to gain control over the forces which were destroying his family.

Joe had taken control of his family because he was the only one who released his anger. This gave him power, however unhealthy it may have been. The only problem was that Joe was too young to be emotionally in charge of his family. He abused his power and his family as well. He hated himself for what he was doing, but he didn't know how to stop. He needed his parents to take control so that he didn't have to.

YOU DON'T HAVE TO BE A VICTIM

Ask yourself these questions:

- Do you feel like a victim of people or circumstances around you?
- Do you ever feel weak or powerless against the forces that seem to control your life?
- Do you find yourself unable to express any feelings at all?
- Do you find yourself exploding in anger over little things?
- Do you often feel irritable and aggravated for no apparent reason?
- Are you intimidated by the anger of others?
- Do you feel guilty every time you express your anger?
- Do you have violent dreams?
- Are you afraid that if you let your anger out, you might hurt someone?
- Are you afraid that if you really let yourself feel all of your emotions, you will go crazy or even die?
- Do you believe you just don't have any feelings?
- Do you find yourself in conflict with others too much of the time?
- Are you in conflict with yourself?
- Have you given up on trying to live your dreams?

- Do you feel that the abuse or neglect you experienced in the past has set the course for your life and there's nothing you can do about it?
- Do you sometimes wish someone would come and take care of you and make everything okay?
- Do you wish your anger would go away and never come back?
- Do you live in constant fear of something awful happening?
- Do you sometimes have the thought, "If life is this awful, why am I here?"

If you answered "Yes" to *any* of these questions, you can benefit from learning about the healthy power of your anger.

Your anger is the strength you need to break free from your feelings of helplessness and powerlessness. Anger is not bad. It is the emotion that comes from inside you when you know something isn't right. It is the motivation to make things better in your life.

In this book, I will be emphasizing the following ideas:

- *Anger is an emotion, and all emotions are okay.*
- *We have to have anger to survive in a world that is sometimes dangerous, abusive and cruel.*
- *Anger is a powerful feeling which is natural and exists only for the purpose of self-preservation.*
- *Anger is emotional energy which we can use to create and maintain healthy boundaries.*
- *Anger is one of the ways the nurturing inner parent protects the vulnerable inner child.*
- *Anger does not have to lead to aggression or attack.*
- *Anger doesn't have to hurt anyone!*
- *Anger is energy and strength to be used for protection.*
- *Anger is based on love.*

1

Anger:
The Protective Shield

A feeling of safety and security is important to all of us. Anger is one of the feelings that comes when our safety is threatened. Fear is the other feeling.

Fear is the natural first-level reaction to threat. Anger is the secondary, protective response. Without anger as an ally, we are only afraid.

We usually think of protection in terms of physical safety. Guns, alarm systems and the martial arts are all for the purpose of protection. In this chapter we will talk about a different kind of protection, one that arises naturally from deep within our emotional self.

I'M SO MAD I COULD LIFT A CHEVY!

I remember reading a news account of a woman who lifted the front end of an automobile off her son, who was

1

pinned underneath. Apparently he had been working on the car and it slipped off the jack and fell on him. Let's run the camera back a bit. We'll try to figure out what happened that gave this woman the strength to perform a feat that seemed physically impossible. Let's call the mom Joyce and her son Tommy.

When Tommy was born, Joyce was overwhelmed with love for the soft, vulnerable bundle of life and mystery that had somehow grown and emerged from within her womb. Her love for her son was natural and powerful, coming from deep within her, through no effort of her own. When Tommy was four, his father died, and Joyce's love grew even stronger.

As she watched him grow, she had to let Tommy go in some ways to allow him to explore, to learn and develop. Her protective instinct never diminished, however, because it came straight from her love. She was always aware of where he was and what he was doing. She was determined to be available if he ever needed her.

Joyce had just finished the dishes from lunch and was considering an afternoon nap. After all, it was Saturday and she had worked hard all week. She went to the back of the house to see how Tommy was coming along on the repair work he was doing on his car. She could hear the sound of the ratchet wrench and smell the mixture of oil and gas as she opened the door into the garage. At 18, it seemed Tommy was more interested in that car than anything in the world — except maybe girls.

As she put one foot into the garage, she saw the car jack leaning dangerously, about to drop thousands of pounds of metal onto the head and upper body of her son. It was as if time stood still. All of the love she had ever felt for her son came flooding to the surface and turned to fear. She barely had a chance to say "Tommy!" when it was too late. The jack slipped, dropping the chassis and exposed metal wheel rim onto her beloved son's chest and shoulder.

There were no thoughts in Joyce's mind. Something deep inside her screamed, "No!" in response to her fear. She rushed to the front bumper of the beat-up old Chevy.

She never questioned whether she could lift the car or whether she should call for help. All she knew was that her Tommy was in trouble and he needed her. Something tremendously powerful came from deep within her and surged through her hands, arms, shoulders and back. Joyce knew somehow that she could not let that car crush her son.

All of a sudden the car was her enemy, and she channeled all her anger into removing it from the vulnerable body of her only son. The anger that surged through Joyce's body was against everything that had ever threatened her son in any way. It was a primal raging at the threat of losing someone she had brought into the world, nurtured and raised.

She lifted the car just enough for Tommy to slide out, badly bruised but with no permanent injury. Joyce then released the bumper, letting the car fall. Exhausted and relieved, she went to her son. Later she remembered almost nothing of what happened. She had no idea how she had been able to lift that much weight. She knew she could never do it again . . . unless . . .

Joyce demonstrated the physical empowerment of anger, motivated by the tremendous love she had for her son. If she had been depressed and lethargic, out of touch with her emotions, her son could have died under that old Chevy.

RAPE? NOT THIS LADY!

Geneva had been asleep for several hours when she awoke with a strange man's hand over her mouth.

As a therapist, Geneva dealt with rape and incest victims as a standard part of her practice. One thing each of these clients had in common was a problem dealing with and expressing their anger. She didn't spend much time thinking about her clients. However, with this strange man in her room in the middle of the night, the only thought that went through her mind was, "Oh, no you don't! *Nobody* is going to do that to *me!*"

Those words never made it out of her mouth. There was a roar of rage and indignation that emanated from deep within her chest and came straight out into the face of the surprised would-be rapist. Her rage was at all the rapists and child molesters who had ever hurt her and those she loved.

The power of the sound and fury that emerged from Geneva seemed to propel the disoriented man out of the room. Without realizing what she was doing, Geneva chased him all the way to the front door of her house.

Her son, who had been awakened by the noise, stopped her just before she bolted into the front yard after him. It was only then that she realized that the intruder had been holding a gun.

"Mom! That man could have killed you!" her son exclaimed, not sure if what he was saying was true. He had never seen such strength and power in his mother — or in anyone else, for that matter. The intruder never had a chance.

Geneva valued herself too highly to even consider for a moment the possibility that she could be violated. Her anger came from awareness of her own inner vulnerability, which she was determined to protect. Through her own therapy, she was in touch with her precious inner child and had made the decision that no one was going to abuse her ever again.

This woman was not a victim. Her fear did not overpower her. Her healthy love for life and her anger literally saved her from being raped and possibly killed.

Geneva was empowered by both her knowledge and her self-love. She knew there was tremendous strength in her because she had experienced it before. As a child, she had been a victim of a violent assault and rape. She had been through years of therapy to resolve the pain and fear that had resulted from this trauma. Claiming her anger had been a significant key to her recovery. She had also seen the power of anger in the recovery of her clients during her past 12 years as a therapist.

Her anger would have been worthless to her if she had not had the experience of loving and appreciating herself. The strength Geneva showed against the intruder is similar to the strength Joyce showed in lifting the car off of her son. It was motivated by love.

If Geneva had felt worthless and bad inside, she might have believed that she deserved punishment. This could have been deadly when she was faced with the rapist in her bedroom. Her fear would have been stronger than her anger, and her power would have been sapped by the fear.

LOVE IS THE FUEL FOR THE FIRE OF ANGER

Even though anger doesn't look very loving when it comes out, it seems that we get the most angry where there is the most love. Any police officer will tell you that the most dangerous calls are domestic ones. We get angry at those we love because they have such tremendous power to hurt us. We give them that power when we choose to love them.

Each of us was born with a tremendous need for love. This need is just as strong as the need for food and shelter. If we are deprived of love, food or shelter, the results are the same. We get physically or emotionally sick. In some cases we die.

It was our parents' job to meet these needs. However, our need for love was never perfectly met, no matter how wonderful our parents may have been. They were all human beings.

Because our need for love is never perfectly met, each of us is hurt as a natural part of growing up. This may have been unintentional, as is the case with much abandonment and neglect. Our parents may have had serious problems of their own, however, and they may have deliberately hurt us. We may also have been hurt by other significant caregivers, such as step-parents, uncles, aunts or grandparents.

One way or another, each of us was hurt emotionally as a child because of our tremendous need for love. That's

the heart of the matter, the center of the circle — the
need to love and be loved.

Figure 1.1. The Heart Of The Matter

Look at the diagram in Figure 1.1 and follow the circles
out from the center as a description of emotional development. Imagine yourself starting at the center and growing
outward emotionally. Picture this as spheres rather than
circles, beginning at the center of your being around your
solar plexus and moving out into the world.

The essence of who we are is a vulnerable being who
needs to give and receive love. Hurting is part of loving
and, therefore, it is also a part of living. We are hurt
because of how incredibly vulnerable we are. This is a
natural part of being a human being and living on this
planet. There's nothing wrong with hurting. The important thing is what we do about it.

Face your pain and you are free to do something about
it. Deny your pain and you are powerless to do anything
that might stop the hurting.

Because we are hurt, we learn to fear. We fear being hurt again. Fear is natural. Claim it and it's yours. You are then free to take action to resolve the fearful situation. Deny your fear and you don't have it, it has you. Your actions are then governed by your fear, and you will find yourself feeling like a victim in any fearful situation. By denying or suppressing our fear, we give away all of our power. By claiming and embracing our fear as our own, we claim the power to act and to protect our vulnerable inner child.

Another kind of fear is directed inward toward ourselves. When something bad happens, we often fear that it's our fault. This is what we call shame. The logic seems to go like this: "If something that bad could happen to me, it must mean that there's something wrong with me. Or else why would it have happened?"

THAT'S MY TONGUE ON THAT POLE

It was a typical winter day in Anchorage, Alaska, about 35 degrees below freezing. I was four years old, over at my friend Rusty's house playing in his carport. I had the good fortune of coming from a basically loving family, so I hadn't yet learned of the cruel edges of the world.

In a friendly manner, Rusty invited me to stick out my tongue and put it on his carport pole. Being a daredevil (and also naive), I complied willingly.

Immediately I knew there was something wrong. I hadn't really planned a long relationship with this pole, but it just wouldn't let go of my tongue. I knew I couldn't stay that way for long. So, "Rrriiip!" and I was free . . . sort of.

I still remember how the top layer of my tongue looked, staring back at me from that pole as if to say, "I belong in your mouth!"

I felt real bad. My tongue was bleeding, and my feelings were hurting even worse than my tongue. It never occurred to me to get mad. I had never learned how. Instead, I felt bad about myself.

Looking back, I can remember thinking, "Why would he do something so mean to me? There must be something wrong with me or else he wouldn't have done that!" Instead of turning outward in anger, I turned inward and questioned myself. This is how shame begins. My childhood experience proved to be an excellent example of the inner-directed fear that, "There's something wrong with me."

Figure 1.2. The Circle Of Protection

Take a look at Figure 1.2. You can see that a new circle has been added, representing the sphere of protection and defense. Anger is the emotion of protection and defense.

Without it, all we can do is hide, withdraw and question ourselves.

Let's summarize this view of emotional development. Because we need so much love, we get hurt. Because we are hurt, we fear being hurt again or we fear that there's something wrong with us inside. We can't face the world like this, so we develop some kind of protection or defense. This is where anger comes in.

There's the connection between ange. and love. Originally, anger is based on a love for comfort and pleasure and a desire to avoid pain. Later, as our love grows and becomes more complex, our capacity for anger grows as well. As adults, of course, we often get angry as a result of our love for others and a desire to protect them from pain.

Imagine the vulnerable core within yourself, located at your solar plexus, just about in the middle of your body. In this most vulnerable place inside your emotional self, your greatest need is to love and be loved. The next layer of emotion surrounding this sphere is your emotional memory of all the pain you have suffered in your love relationships. Then comes your fear sphere — fear of more pain or fear that you are unlovable or worthless.

Then comes the sphere of anger. Your anger may be at others, at yourself or both. That's your way of responding to the fear and pain underneath.

Right now you might be thinking, "I don't know what this guy is talking about. I can't find any of those feelings in myself." When anger doesn't do the trick for protecting us from pain and fear, our mind comes to the rescue with the great weapon called denial. If you want to get in touch with and learn about your feelings, you will have to learn to lay down your weapons against them.

BUT I'M AFRAID OF MY ANGER

Most anger is expressed in unhealthy ways. For this reason, there are many negative beliefs about anger. Here are a few I have heard:

- If I start showing my anger, no one will like me.
- Every time I have been angry in the past, someone has been hurt.
- If I let this out, I'm afraid I might hurt someone.
- I don't have any anger. I decided that a long time ago.
- I wouldn't want my children to learn that from me!
- Why can't we just solve these problems rationally?
- Can't I just talk about my feelings in a calm, adult manner?
- The world would be a better place if everyone would just control themselves.
- Every time I get angry, I start crying. I hate that.
- I'm afraid if I really start letting my feelings out, I'll never stop.
- There's something really bad, even evil inside me. If I let my anger out, there's no telling what would happen.
- I hate anger. When my father got angry, my mother got beaten.

These thoughts and beliefs can rob us of our ability to feel our feelings. Like denial, they are weapons to fight off emotions. The only problem is that, along with our emotions, they often kill our strength and power for recovery and success.

Healing is natural. When there is nothing wrong, nothing interfering, we heal automatically. When we suppress anger, we also suppress our fear, our pain and — yes, our love.

Love is the source of healing, and suppressing it slows down or stops the healing process.

Just as love was the source of the power experienced by Joyce and Geneva, it is the source we need to heal and empower ourselves and our lives.

My anger is for my protection, and I deserve to feel safe and secure.

2

Buried Anger Just Won't Stay Down

IF YOU CAN'T SAY SOMETHING NICE . . .

We start learning to bury anger in our childhood. There are some sure-fire ways to get children to suppress their anger. Following are some scenarios that are guaranteed to lead to buried anger:

1. Our parents suppressed their own anger. No one ever raised their voice, but there was a very powerful non-verbal message that said, "Stay in control. We don't act that way here." There was an even stronger message that said, "If you act ugly, we won't love you." What choice does a child have?

2. We were abused physically, which was a result of the abuser's anger. We learned from this that anger is awful, that it causes the type of fear and pain we felt

when we were abused. The big fear goes something like this: "If I get angry, I will be just like my abuser. By controlling my own anger, I can be sure I will never hurt people like that." We therefore suppress our anger to avoid causing pain and fear for others as well as for ourselves.

3. We were victims of sexual or physical abuse and blamed ourselves, either partly or completely. This leads to shame and the basic belief that accompanies this feeling which is, "I have no right to be angry." As we discussed earlier, shame is inner-directed fear and leads to a deep feeling of worthlessness. This leads to an indirect and yet very powerful suppression of anger.

4. Mom or Dad specifically punished us for the expression of anger in any form. "Go to your room until you can act right!" The message to the child is clear: "I'm not supposed to get mad. Mom and Dad won't love me if I act like that." We may also have been physically punished or abused for showing anger. This only has to happen once, in some cases, for the message to come through loud and clear that anger is bad and must be buried.

5. It wasn't just anger that was hidden in our home. It was all emotions. The fear of anger was so great that all of the other feelings were suppressed along with it. The message here is that all feelings are bad. The only problem is that each of us knows at some level that our feelings are part of who we are. Suppression of feelings in this way leads to a feeling of worthlessness and low self-esteem. We just can't suppress our feelings and get away with it.

COMPULSIONS, ADDICTIONS AND OTHER SMOKE SCREENS

Without anger, we have to develop other ways of protecting ourselves. If we are not going to stand our ground and express our feelings, our only option is to withdraw or create some kind of distraction. Some skills for withdrawal are necessary and healthy, and we will talk about that in a later chapter. Distractions are simply a form of denial.

Compulsions and addictions are great "smoke screens" or distractions from the real issues in our lives. If we get involved enough in the addiction or compulsion, our anger gets buried under all the new problems resulting from our unhealthy behavior.

Anger does not go away. We can bury it for a while, but it never stays buried. It's only a matter of time before it shows up in a violent rage, a major illness, depression or suicide. When anger is buried, it always has a victim.

We tend to react to buried anger in one or both of the following two ways:

1. *We get sick.* Depression can result from buried anger, and that reduces the effectiveness of our immune system. Physical illness can result from the depression or from the stress caused by the suppressed emotion. The anger does not get expressed, but it makes its presence known. This is sometimes called internalized anger or self-hatred, leading to suicidal thoughts or suicidal behavior.

2. *We explode in fits of anger.* These explosions can range all the way from violent rages to minor temper tantrums. The main point is that we are not in control, and we do things we do not intend to do. We often hurt ourselves and others when our buried anger erupts to the surface. This is the "pressure cooker" syndrome we talked about earlier.

When anger is dealt with in these ways, it always has a victim. Compulsive and addictive behaviors can develop in either of the above scenarios. Keeping feelings inside doesn't feel good. It hurts. Drug and alcohol addiction often results from self-medicating the pain which is caused by suppressed emotions.

Rageaholics may use substances or compulsive behaviors to try to control their rage. "I am so relaxed and pleasant when I drink. I only fly into those rages when I'm sober." This is a statement from a woman in denial, using alcohol to attempt to control her rage.

I'M SURE I COULD STOP DRINKING IF I COULD JUST STOP GETTING ANGRY

Clarice's presenting problem was her rage. She would usually start out being upset over some trivial detail around the house and eventually drag in 17 years of her husband's inadequacy and attack him with it.

"Everything will be going just fine," Clarice explained while staring out the window of my office, "and then I get this feeling. I start out complaining, and the next thing I know I'm screaming at the top of my lungs and throwing things at Foster. I've even hit him in the face with my fists a few times. I don't know why I do that.

"But you know, after I have a couple of glasses of wine, I just calm right down. He even brings me a glass of wine when he gets home sometimes. I guess he's figured it out by now."

Without realizing it, Clarice had mixed two very serious addictions. She was addicted to rage and to alcohol, and the two problems were feeding into each other. She was in total denial about her alcoholism.

"My drinking is not a problem. I'd be in bad shape without it though. I can quit any time I want to but I have to learn to control my anger first." Clarice had a way of talking that made it very clear it would be pointless to argue with her.

I decided to use her belief that the alcohol was not a problem as a way to get past her defenses.

"I'd like you to abstain from drinking while you are in therapy, Clarice. You'll have greater mental clarity, and also make much more progress that way. I'll give you some other ways to control your anger, besides drinking."

It was a long shot, but I knew I couldn't help her if she continued drinking while I was working with her.

"Sure, that's no problem. Like I said, I can quit any time I want to." She squirmed a little when she said this. I think her body was telling me that her words were not totally true. Clarice's struggle with her rage proved more than she was ready for. Without the alcohol for self-medication, she found herself in either violent rages or serious depression. Her marriage was collapsing rapidly and she found herself unable to keep a job.

Her commitment to recovery was not strong, since she had not acknowledged her powerlessness over alcohol. She returned to her drinking. It was an excellent distraction from her emotional problems, and she also happened to be addicted to alcohol.

This woman was not ready to remove the distraction by dealing with her addiction, so she didn't deal with her buried anger. But it continued to deal with her. It just wouldn't stay down.

I ONLY GET MAD WHEN I'M DRUNK

There are also many cases in which alcohol is the trigger to release the rage. This usually occurs when the person can't let go emotionally. The drinking is an effort to ease the stress of emotional suppression. Extreme suppression often leads to rage. The alcohol provides a false sense of comfort, allowing a release of the rage. The results can be devastating.

This type of problem needs little explanation. Almost all of us know of someone who is only angry and abusive after having a few drinks.

In such cases, the alcoholism treatment must occur before or along with the psychotherapy. The distractions of substance abuse provide a very effective mask for emotional problems. If these addiction issues are not addressed, the emotional issues will never be resolved.

A LONG-OVERDUE TEMPER TANTRUM

Remember Joe, Sam's son, whom we were discussing earlier? His alcoholism was the first problem addressed when he went into treatment.

Focusing on his alcoholism gave Joe some security, as drinking was something he thought he might be able to understand and possibly even control. His rage, however,

seemed to be too big for him to handle, and he was terrified of facing the pain that was behind it.

Since he was young and the alcoholism was not chronic,
Joe was able to commit to his recovery program early in
treatment. Being away from both his family and alcohol,
he was free to begin facing his emotions in a safe environment. He finally began to deal with his rage.

Like most people, Joe was afraid at first. In the stark,
unadorned seclusion room at the hospital, he knelt on the
end of the mat. He just couldn't seem to get into it. He
kept talking, trying to avoid facing the anger and pain he
knew was there inside.

"I'm just not angry," he explained, trying not to look at
me. "Now that I've got a handle on my drinking, I want to
get out of here and live a normal life."

"What about your parents?" I asked, knowing he hadn't
dealt with his feelings toward them.

"I never want to see them again," he replied in a voice
too calm for such a statement. "Oh, maybe I'll see my dad.
I need his help to get a car and a job." He grew quiet, and
I knew by the look in his eyes that his thoughts had
returned to Mom.

"Why don't you just lie down on the mat and relax for
a minute, Joe." He followed my suggestion, and I lowered
my voice a little to see if I could get him into his feelings.

"Close your eyes and think of all the reasons you don't
want to see your mother ever again."

I could see that he became immediately anxious, so I
asked what he was thinking. He recounted memories of
his mother walking around in her underwear in front of
him and sometimes allowing him to see her nude.

"That confused me. I was attracted to her, but I knew
it was wrong. She kept doing it over and over for all those
years. I really hate her for that."

His rage was beginning to surface. Usually at this point
he would have suppressed his emotions and found some
distraction, like drinking.

I said softly, "Let that out. You don't need to carry that
pain, confusion and anger around anymore. Just pound

the mat with both hands and kick with both feet." I was suggesting the "temper tantrum" technique. He tried a little bit of pounding, then stopped. "What happened?" I asked, knowing the answer to my own question. "I don't know. I guess I don't want to hurt her." "She's not here," I replied. "This is for you. You won't hurt her, you will only help yourself by unloading some of the baggage you've been carrying all these years.

"Hit the mat again, and this time kick with your feet and see if you can shake off some of the guilt you've been feeling for being attracted to your mother. As you pound and kick, yell, 'It's my fault! It's my fault!' "

He didn't follow my suggestions. But all of a sudden, his rage exploded. He was kicking and pounding with tremendous strength. After about five seconds of this, he opened his mouth and roared.

With that roar, Joe was releasing 20 years of pain and anger. The walls seemed to vibrate with the intensity of what was happening in that room. I had to hold the mat to keep it from flying out from under him. He was "losing control" in a safe, protected environment. There were no victims.

When he was out of breath, he looked at me and said, "That feels good. Can I do it again?"

I smiled. "Go for it!"

This may sound strange, but I was actually excited and relieved to see Joe doing this. I knew that if his rage had stayed buried within him, he could have killed — himself, someone else or both. I knew that by releasing the rage in this controlled, therapeutic environment, he was saving his own life and possibly the lives of others.

Joe had been having recurrent dreams of killing and mutilating women. He had attempted suicide several times. He had threatened both his parents' lives. I was seeing first-hand the emergence of the subconscious rage behind his desire to kill and to die. It was not ugly or frightening to me. It was like removing a malignant tumor and giving someone a new chance to live.

Now Joe could learn to express his anger in healthy ways and to establish boundaries for his protection. With the rage behind it, Joe's anger had always been distorted and dangerous. Now that he had removed the distraction of alcohol and was releasing his rage, he had a chance to get angry and express it in a healthy way, with no victims.

YOUR MIND IS NO PLACE TO HIDE FROM YOUR FEELINGS

One of the most socially acceptable ways to suppress emotions is to "Be rational." That is, "Don't feel, think," or "Use your head!" The rational, intellectual world provides safety and predictability for those who feel lost in the world of emotions. The only problem is those darned old feelings just won't go away.

Marcus worked with his mind. As an engineer and mathematician, he spent most of his waking hours exploring the rational and precise realms of his intellect.

Sitting in his office having a cup of coffee on a Friday morning, he found himself thinking about his many accomplishments. He had received promotions every time he had been up for them. He had also received consistent and substantial pay raises. He was well thought of among his colleagues. That's where his self-esteem stopped. Apart from his work, he considered himself a failure.

Harry came into Marcus' office and asked if he had finished the prospectus. Coming out of his daydream, Marcus remembered that he was behind schedule and the pressure was on. With Harry standing there looking at him, he was starting to get hot and he could feel the sweat forming on his brow. He had no excuse to offer his boss.

This had been happening all too frequently lately. He mumbled some feeble explanation to Harry. He noticed the older man shaking his head as he walked out the door.

Something was wrong. Suddenly it seemed that the one area of his life which had been stable and satisfying was beginning to show signs of strain. If he started falling apart at work, his whole life would be a shambles.

At home Marcus was used to feelings of inadequacy and tension. His daughter had been struggling with drug addiction for over two years now. His wife Sarah had been talking of divorce almost daily. The fighting between his wife and daughter had grown steadily worse, to the point that Sarah had put locks on her bedroom door to keep her daughter out.

Now, sitting in his office, he found that the powerless and helpless feelings he had at home were beginning to surface in his professional life. Marcus had always been considered brilliant by his peers. For years they had brought their most intricate and challenging problems to him, knowing the power of his mind.

But lately he was finding it difficult to concentrate on the simplest of tasks. Worst of all, he could no longer make decisions. He found himself going into a panic as his mind raced from one thought to another. He couldn't put information together and draw any type of meaningful conclusions.

When he came to me for counseling about his family problems, all Marcus was able to do was gather information. He took notes throughout the session and didn't seem to really understand anything I said. His intellect was clouded as a result of a lifetime of emotional suppression.

It was as if the unexpressed emotion had built and grown like a thunderhead to the point that it expanded to his brain and clouded his thinking. He lived constantly with an unexplained mixture of fear and tension, and was stuck in cycles of repetitive thoughts.

He kept repeating that he never got angry.

When Marcus finally received inpatient treatment, it was not his decision. He was no longer capable of making decisions or controlling his emotions. Sarah recognized what was needed when she found her husband sitting at his desk at 5:00 am on a Sunday morning, crying over a business document.

All he could say was, "I don't know. I don't know. I don't know." This was his answer to all the unanswered questions in his life.

Why had his father locked him in the basement every time he had shown any sign of emotion? Why had his mother slapped him so hard in front of all those people the one and only time he had expressed his anger? Why were his only happy memories associated with school and his academic accomplishments? Why was his life falling apart? Why couldn't he think clearly anymore? He didn't even know why he was crying. He just did not know.

It wasn't intellectual knowledge that Marcus needed. He needed the wisdom that could only come from fully experiencing his emotions.

FEELINGS ARE JUST LIKE VEGETABLES

Vegetables and feelings are best when they are fresh. As a matter of fact, they are downright good for us when they are fresh.

"Ouch!" That's one of the freshest ways to express pain. Other simple and to-the-point ways of expressing feelings go like this:

"That hurts!"
"I'm hurting."
"I'm scared."
"I'm angry."
"I'm happy."
"I love you."
"Great!"
"Fantastic!"

These simple, current expressions of emotions are healthy and productive. They let the listener know exactly what is going on. These are statements we can make to let our feelings out while they are still fresh.

We all know what happens when we leave vegetables too long without using them. They get smelly and they are bad for us. It's the same with feelings.

The longer we leave our feelings inside without expressing them, the more unpleasant they become. When old buried feelings come out, they tend to make our bodies shake and sweat and our eyes and noses tend to run — almost as if we were smelling old decomposed vegetables. Buried feelings, like buried vegetables, don't just lie there. They get hot and generate energy, which has to come out one way or another. If we keep them inside, they might burn holes in our stomachs (ulcers). There is some evidence that cancer, a kind of overburning of cells, is connected to suppressed anger.

When vegetables go bad, we need to uncover them and use them in a compost where they will do some good. When our buried feelings start to cause problems, they need to come out. It's the only way. We can't pour something down there to kill them (like alcohol or some other chemical). That just causes new problems. We can't just work a little harder, exercise a little more or read a book about self-control. These are only temporary solutions.

If we do get caught up in trying these many and creative ways of avoiding our feelings, they just get hotter and hotter in there and cause all kinds of problems.

I CAN'T STAND TO BE ALONE

Much of what we do each day is a distraction from our feelings.

Other people are the greatest distraction of all if we choose to use them in that way. This is one of the "great escapes" of co-dependency. Fear of being alone is the fear of not having distractions from our feelings.

What if you were to just stop?

What if you were to sit still for a while? Why not?

What if you were to practice the skill of being okay alone, so it wasn't frightening to you any more?

What would happen if all your going, doing and thinking just stopped?

You would start to feel. Feelings. That's all that would be left. Take away the thinking and doing, and the feelings rise to the surface. After all, each of us is made up of thinking, doing and feeling.

Usually we wait until life grabs us by the collar or the throat and throws us to the ground before we really start to face our feelings. Even then, we only face them until we can get moving again. Why is that?

Perhaps it is because we have all been hurt, and we don't really want to face that. None of us had a perfect childhood. The rest of our lives have also had some rough spots, so we've been hurt some more. We may also feel shame and guilt about ourselves and our behavior.

So what do we do? We can't sit around in self-pity all the time. We can't blame our parents for all our problems. Or even if we do, where's that going to get us? They are not likely to come and make it all better at this point.

Most of the time, we just keep on trucking. We just keep on. We do what we know how to do. That's just it. We don't do what we don't know how to do.

If we don't know how to be alone with our feelings, we will keep burying them until they get too hot and smelly and we are forced to deal with them because of some kind of crisis. This is how we become "crisis junkies." We need the crises for the emotional release they always bring.

Then, as soon as the crisis is over, we will bury our feelings away again, not realizing they will be even hotter and smellier next time they come up. As long as we are alive, our feelings will not die. So why try to bury them?

Experience your feelings (and your vegetables) while they are fresh. They are good for you!

My anger is part of who I am. By claiming and experiencing my anger, I am adding to my inner strength and self-esteem.

3

Breaking Free From The Passivity Prison

To be passive means not to be active. If we are passive, we let things happen instead of making things happen. If we are passive, we don't do, we are done to. This leads to the feeling of being a victim of the people and circumstances around us. Nobody likes to be a victim.

We feel like a victim when we are stuck in our own passivity prison — afraid to act, afraid not to act, paralyzed by fear.

As infants we were all passive. We had no choice. We were just not capable of very much action. We could cry, soil our diapers, rattle our rattle, make gurgling noises and smile. That's about it. As infants we were passive recipients of what the world offered us, like it or not.

We were born as innocent, open children. When we were hurt or neglected, there wasn't much we could do about it. We could cry, but sometimes we were even punished for that. This is the first experience any of us had of being a victim. As children, we were victims of an imperfect world that sometimes has sharp and cruel edges. This is nobody's fault, it's just the way it is. We need to acknowledge this fact and deal with it, so we don't continue to feel like victims throughout our adult lives.

I'M HERE, YOU'RE HERE. . . .
WHY CAN'T I TOUCH YOU?

Paul was the kind of guy who looked as if he had it all together. Handsome, slim, a good dresser, he had a ready smile and a handshake when we met. He was a master at making a good impression and helping others to feel at ease. You can imagine my surprise when he said to me, "I don't know who I am. I look inside here and I don't find anything."

He had heard me speak on co-dependency a couple of weeks prior to our meeting, and this was his first experience with counseling or therapy of any kind.

"My son hates me. I can't seem to get close to him, even though I want that more than anything else in the world. He and my wife are close and I feel cut off from both of them. I know I'm supposed to express my feelings, but I don't seem to have any. I don't know what to do, so I don't do anything."

It was only after our seventh session that Paul began to talk about what really bothered him the most.

He had just come home from an ordinary day at the job he despised. His 14-year-old son Michael was there, watching television. For some reason he was furious at his son and began looking for a cause to justify his anger. "Aahh! His room. That's a sure-fire reason to feel this way. I'll bet it's filthy!" These were Paul's barely conscious thoughts as he strode with determination to Michael's room.

At work Paul was a follower. He never took initiative and rarely made decisions. If he did actually decide on something, he rarely followed through. He never expressed his opinions. He didn't agree with all the decisions of his superiors but he kept these thoughts to himself. He found himself feeling angry and frustrated most of the time. He kept these feelings to himself at work, but somehow at home with his son they just seemed to erupt.

It started slowly, as it always did. "Michael, I'm sick and tired of looking at your filthy room! Turn off that stupid boob tube and get in there and clean it up!"

"It's clean enough for me. Besides, this is my favorite program, I'll do it after it's over." Michael was not worried. It had been several months since his dad had been really tough with him, and most of the time he could get away with that kind of back-talk.

Paul could feel the slow burn in his gut turning into a boil. He had to put up with whatever came his way at work, but he didn't have to put up with it in his own home. Besides this kid had been treating him like dirt lately, and he just wasn't going to put up with it! Without thinking, he moved rapidly to Michael's chair and jerked him up by his arm. Michael's anger was not so deeply buried as his father's. As a matter of fact, it seemed as if he had taken the job of expressing his father's unexpressed rage.

"Get your hands off me!" Michael screamed, with as much fear as anger. His father had never gone quite this far before.

That was it for Paul. He had been ordered around by his father the whole time he was growing up, and now as a man he took orders all day every day at work. No way was this 14-year-old kid going to give him orders and get away with it. For just a moment, Paul forgot that this was the son he had always loved and cared for. The rage boiling inside him erupted into an explosion.

Paul hit his son with his free hand so hard that Michael spun around two times before hitting the book case. The powerful release of energy felt good to Paul. He had been building up to that breaking point for a long time. He was almost beginning to enjoy the feeling of relief when he realized what he had done. His wife had come into the room and was holding her son in her arms, looking at Paul with disbelief and pain in her eyes.

Suddenly Paul snapped and his usual "nice guy" perspective returned. At once he was afraid and horrified at what he had done. As soon as he saw that Michael was all right, he left the room. Alone in his study Paul turned his rage on himself. For a moment he considered suicide, but quickly ruled that out. He just didn't feel strong enough. Inside himself he was shutting down again, squelching all of the emotion that had just welled up in him and exploded in violence. He had felt so good for a moment, having released his pent-up emotions. But this only added to his guilt now. How could he dare to feel so good after hitting his own son?

Paul couldn't think of anything to do. He sat, frozen, and stared at the room without seeing anything.

He wanted to apologize, to take back what he had done. He wished he could somehow turn back the clock and control the insidious rage that had made him hurt someone he loved so much.

But Paul did not do anything. He was paralyzed . . . stuck. He was back in the passivity prison, locked away for his crime. The jailer for this prison always kept a close watch on the prisoner. It was himself.

Perhaps the saddest part of this scenario was that Paul had suppressed all of his other feelings along with his anger. Remember the concentric circles of emotion from Chapter One? It's as if Paul pushed in on the anger circle, and in the process closed off his fear, his pain and even his love. This is why he was sitting in my office saying he had no feelings at all. Since he was not aware of his feelings, he had no sense of who he was as a person. In a sense, our feelings are who we are inside. When we deny them, we are denying ourselves.

ANGER WITH A VICTIM JUST DOESN'T WORK

The only way Paul had ever broken out of his passivity was in an explosion of anger. His anger had always had a victim, so he could not accept it as a means of breaking free. He was stuck. His frustration always drove him to the point of anger. Tired of being a passive wimp, tired of people telling him what to do, tired of having no control over his life, he would explode and immediately regret it. His anger had always hurt someone, and this went against his nature. He had been taught to be nice to others and he sincerely wanted to be a good person. This left him with the continuing problem of how to become an active participant in his own life.

THE OPPOSITE OF PASSIVE IS ACTIVE — NOT AGGRESSIVE

Action. That's what Paul needed. He needed only to decide on one small step and then to take it. There are many ways out of the passivity prison, and they all involve taking some form of direct positive action.

Paul signed up for a self-help seminar. He had seen his son growing up and his chance at a relationship slipping away. He was determined that his son would not end up hating him the way he had always hated his own father. He knew that the problem was his. That is what prevented him from being a chronic abuser.

We either act or react. If we don't take action, we are left with no choice but to react to someone else's action. This is fine if we like what they do. If not, we may feel like a victim. And yet it was often our choice not to act in the first place.

YOU MAKE THE DECISION AND I'LL SHOOT IT DOWN

"Where do you want to eat tonight, honey?" It seems like an innocent enough question.

"Oh, I don't know, why don't you decide?"

"Okay. I've been thinking about Mexican food all day. Let's try that new restaurant out by the mall."

The first shot is about to be fired. "No, I don't think I want all that greasy food in my stomach. The last time I ate Mexican food I tasted it for hours afterward." Gotcha.

Slightly wounded but willing to push onward, Keith makes another suggestion. "Well, there's always Cassaway's downtown. We could get one of their spinach salads." Unaware of what she's doing, Jill takes a bead on Keith's new suggestion. She has it in her sights, and, "I'm tired of Cassaway's. Besides downtown is depressing now that all those businesses have closed." Another direct hit.

Wounded, and beginning to consider a counter-offensive, Keith has not really figured out what is going on. "Well, if we don't go downtown and patronize their restaurants, we are just adding to the problem you're complaining about." Angry, but not sure why, Keith is losing his appetite.

"I'm not complaining. I was just making an observation." ("Who, me? I didn't fire that shot!") Jill is covering herself well.

Unwilling to be an open target again, Keith takes a new tactic. "Well, I'm going to Mario's for lasagna. If you want to come along, that's fine. I'm tired of arguing." Finally someone is taking some action.

In the above example, Jill is being passive/aggressive, which requires that she take no direct action but indirectly attack Keith for the action he takes or proposes to take. If Keith had continued with his counter-offensive, both would have been caught up in a destructive battle in which neither knew what was really going on. The resolution occurred because action was taken. The opposite of passive is active, not aggressive.

Keith's action was a good example of anger expressed in a healthy manner. He decided not to counter-attack, even though he was getting angry. To be aggressive (or passive/ aggressive) would have been an unhealthy expression of anger.

Anger does not have to result in aggression. It can be channeled into appropriate healthy action. This is the solution to passivity.

A LEGEND IN HIS OWN MIND

Secretly Paul was a very powerful man. It was such a well-kept secret that no one but Paul even knew of his power. Most of the time he wasn't even aware of it himself. But in his dreams, and sometimes in waking fantasies, Paul did amazing things. He owned his own imaginary multi-million-dollar business. Every one of his employees feared and respected him. When he spoke, everyone listened. When he had a need, everyone jumped to meet it. The love and admiration he desired and missed in his real life were the main focus of his fantasy life.

Sometimes Paul saw himself as a pioneer in the old west named Seth. With his brave and undaunted leadership, he and his wife and son forged a place for themselves in the untamed wilderness. Wild animals, thieves, tornadoes, floods and dust storms could not stand in the way of the powerful and determined Seth. Quick, accurate decisions in the face of life-threatening situations were second nature to this imaginary identity he had created. As Seth, Paul was happier than he had ever been in his life. But the painful difference between Seth and Paul actually made things worse in Paul's real life.

After a thrilling afternoon of conquering the untamed wilderness as Seth, Paul's return to his own life was depressing. His self-esteem was lower after each fantasy trip. Paul didn't like Paul. But he liked power.

THERE'S NOTHING WRONG WITH POWER

Paul didn't like himself in real life because he didn't think he had any power. He couldn't make decisions or take action unless he knew it was approved and recommended by someone else. His eruptions of anger made him feel powerful, but he hated the results of his aggression. He did not know how to release his anger without being aggressive and hurting someone, so he suppressed it, along with his power.

Paul was kneeling on the mat, looking at the dark blue pillow in front of him as if it held some hidden mystery which both frightened and fascinated him. His body was rigid with the restraint and tension that had prevented him from taking initiative all his life. His struggle was because of his frustration and desire to be free — to act, to decide and to feel.

With fists clenched, he raised his arms straight over his head and came down hard on the pillow. He was using the anger release technique I call the "power position." I had given him some phrases to use, but he chose to remain silent. I encouraged him to hit the pillow again. He was starting to shake a little now, and I knew some of his pent-up emotions were breaking through.

Thunk! A pause, with breath sucked between clenched teeth. And then, thunk! thunk! thunk! thunk! thunk! Paul was starting to sob now, but he wasn't letting go yet. A few tears fell.

"Can you feel your strength?" I asked, knowing the answer.

"Yes," he whispered, "but it's scary."

"You aren't hurting anyone here, Paul. You're breaking out of the fear and self-hatred that have kept you locked away from those you love. Your anger is your ally, your strength. Get angry at the feeling of being stuck and cut off from others. Get angry at the fear that keeps you from taking initiative and making decisions. It's time for you to help yourself."

Thud! Thud! This time his blows to the pillow were even stronger than before. Again he started to sob and stopped hitting the pillow. I encouraged him to relax and let the feelings come out, but he sucked them back as soon as he could. When I suggested that he give the pillow another shot or two, he replied with a deep breath, "That's enough for now. It's amazing I was even able to feel that much."

Back in his chair, facing the "empty" chair holding the image and perception of his father, Paul was different. He told his father that he was giving him back his passivity and rigid control over his emotions. He made the decision to give up his father as a role model, once and for all. Having just pounded a pillow and cried in front of a therapy group of six people and a therapist, his emotions were on the surface. I could tell he meant what he was saying. His father would never have done what he was doing. The very act of going through these exercises was a tremendous break with his past and what he had been taught that a "man is supposed to be."

Paul still had a lot of work to do in changing a lifetime of behavior patterns in relationships. But he had done the ground work of releasing his past and claiming his power. He was able to tell his son, face to face, how much he loved him and how sorry he was that he had hit him. He was able to break through the emotional barriers closing himself off from his family.

Some stiffness was still there for Paul and decisions didn't always come easily, but he had started the process of breaking free. Free from his self-made prison of passivity, Paul was now taking powerful action and initiative in making his life what he wanted it to be.

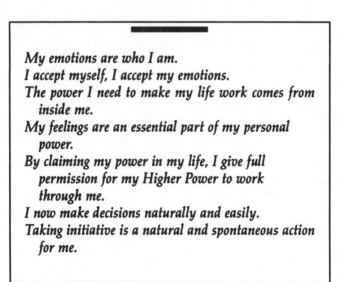

My emotions are who I am.

I accept myself, I accept my emotions.

The power I need to make my life work comes from inside me.

My feelings are an essential part of my personal power.

By claiming my power in my life, I give full permission for my Higher Power to work through me.

I now make decisions naturally and easily.

Taking initiative is a natural and spontaneous action for me.

4

Rage — Anger's Nasty Cousin

A small but fiery woman, Cora had a way of letting you know that she meant what she said. She had not made much progress in dealing with her depression, and she was almost constantly angry. The standard rage release exercises I had used with her just hadn't worked. She was just as angry after hitting the mat as she had been before starting. I felt stumped. The only thing that let me know we might be getting somewhere was that she kept coming back. She was also functioning fairly well since her discharge from the hospital. I certainly wasn't prepared for what she was about to say.

"I just feel like if I could hold my gun right up to his head and pull the trigger, it would be better than sex." I knew she meant it. She was talking about a man she had hated for years, and she carried a loaded revolver with her at all times.

Trying to remain calm, I asked how close she thought she was to doing something like that. She reassured me that it was only a fantasy and that she had too many good reasons not to go through with it. Her statement did tell me something about the depth of her rage, however. She had my attention.

This is the kind of patient a therapist really worries about. She was as potentially suicidal as homicidal, and she carried a loaded weapon. After every session, I got a verbal commitment from her not to kill herself or anyone else and to call me any hour, day or night, if things got really bad.

Cora was seeing a psychiatrist concurrently with her sessions with me and was on appropriate medications to help her control her emotions. She also attended a support group called "Emotions Anonymous," in which she had established some healthy relationships. I still found her progress to be disturbingly slow and sometimes nonexistent. As a therapist, I found myself really stretching to come up with a way to help this woman.

HEALING ON HORSEBACK

"That's the happiest I've ever been in my life." Cora's words grabbed my attention like a passing freight train. She was in the process of sharing more about her past, and I had not heard much from her about happiness. She was telling me about the ten or so years she had spent riding and training horses and competing in barrel-racing.

"It's the only thing I've ever been good at," she said matter-of-factly. The question leaped into my head and out of my mouth without stopping. "Why did you quit riding?"

"Oh, I don't know. Jerry was jealous of all the cowboys and then Sabrina, my favorite mare, died. I just never got back into it." It was obvious, listening to her, that she had allowed her single experience of worth and value to be sabotaged by unhealthy relationships and an inability to deal with her emotions associated with grief and loss.

"We've got to get you on a horse!" I couldn't believe I was saying that, but it was the first real breakthrough possibility I had come up with to help Cora out of her rage and depression. She immediately started giving reasons why she could not get a horse, blaming it on her husband and her circumstances.

"If I told you where you could go tomorrow morning and ride a green-broke gelding, would you do it?" I knew a woman who needed her young horse trained but didn't have the funds to pay for it.

"Yes!" I was seeing the first real enthusiasm I had ever experienced in Cora. I knew she was ready.

We made all the arrangements, and Cora started riding Petrie every day. Her sessions with me went to every other week. The depression lifted, and I saw little sign of the rage. I didn't really understand until one day she told me what had happened.

The day had been one of those that had driven Cora to sleep for 12 to 14 hours and wake up raging at her husband and daughter. Instead of going home, however, she went to the stables, and got on Petrie bareback.

"I love the smell of horses. Something inside me just relaxes when I get around them, especially Petrie. He seems to know what I'm feeling. He likes to blow on me with his big nostrils and he actually licks my hand. This time, when I got on him, he looked back at me over his shoulder without moving. The look of plain old horse love just did it to me. I leaned over and put my arms around his big brown neck and nuzzled my face in his mane. Suddenly something inside me let go, and I started crying. I cried for all the years of hurting when there had been no one there for me. I cried for all the times I had hurt others. Then I cried for no particular reason. I just cried and cried. I must have kept that up for a good 45 minutes. Petrie never moved. I've never known a horse to be so still with someone on their back, especially a young un-trained gelding. It was like he knew what was happening and he was willing to do his part."

Cora comes for counseling on an as-needed basis now. She has her own horse and is riding in some team-roping competition events with her new friends.

This story reminds me of a lesson I keep learning over and over. Everyone is a one-of-a-kind individual. Methods and techniques are great and every therapist needs to have plenty of them. There are times, however, when nothing seems to work and we just have to let the clients help us to help them. Cora helped me to help her by getting on the back of a big hairy four-legged creature who had just what she needed — a quiet stillness and unconditional love.

LETTING RAGE OUT OF THE CAGE

Rage is what gives anger a bad name. It's the "nasty cousin" of anger that is a mixture of old unresolved pain, fear and anger. Look at Figure 4.1. If you collapse the lines between the pain, the fear and the protective layer where anger comes in, mix all that up and leave it there for a long time, you get rage. It's like the old vegetables that were left too long in the refrigerator. It looks bad, smells bad and in some cases is poisonous.

Rage causes problems when it is left inside — and if it is expressed at the wrong time in the wrong way, it causes problems when it is released. Rage is an emotional illness which can lead to serious depression, abusive behavior and even suicidal and homicidal tendencies. It cannot be ignored. It is often a matter of life and death.

Cora hated her rage. This made it stronger. She also hated some other people, which made her rage at herself because she was basically a good person and felt guilty for hating anyone. This is why the standard rage release exercises didn't work for her. The more she raged, the more she raged at herself. This kept her stuck. Petrie the horse taught me that she just needed to grieve in the presence of total acceptance (maybe that's where the term "horse sense" came from). Some people, however, need to get mad — really mad.

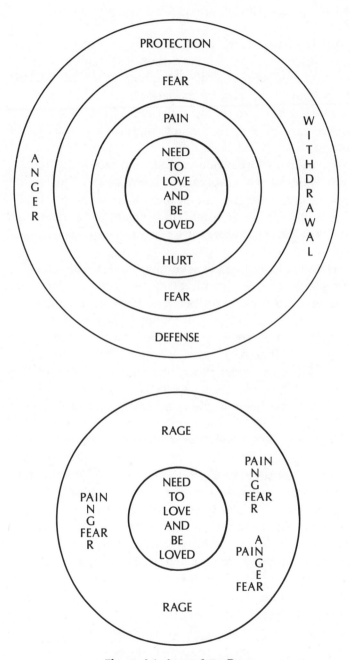

Figure 4.1. Anger Into Rage

RAGE FROM BOUNDARY VIOLATIONS

A crime that horrifies each of us is incest or sexual molestation of any kind. As a therapist, I am amazed at how common sexual abuse is among my clients, particularly those who end up as patients in the hospital. In my work with sexual abuse victims, I have often found rage release to be an important component in the healing process.

When Troy's father had first started molesting him, he didn't know how to respond. He knew he didn't like it, but he also knew he was supposed to do what his father wanted him to do. It wasn't until years later in therapy that Troy realized fathers are not supposed to do that to their sons.

He had been raging for several years. He had lost many jobs and destroyed two marriages with his rage. He had never made a connection between his rage and what his father had done. When it hit him, it was as if his rage came to the surface and said, "Now I have a reason for being here!" It took no coaxing to get Troy to pound the pillow. His rage burst out of its cage with such energy that it took him 45 minutes to recover enough to stand up when he was through. He cried softly for another hour and a half.

The rage release took him straight into the heart of the pain he had been carrying so many years. Until he got past the rage, he could not touch the vulnerable little boy who had been cringing inside in fear ever since his father first touched his genitals with that look in his eye. His healthy expression of anger showed his inner child that what had happened was wrong and that it wasn't his fault. At last he was able to stand up for himself, without shame and without bringing harm to anyone. He claimed his power over his body and his right to be treated with respect.

When a child's tender, sensitive body is violated, particularly by a parent or primary caregiver, the emotional wound inflicted is deep. Recovery is involved and complex, and it cannot be rushed. Rage and anger work may be a necessary part of the process, and it may not be indicated at all. It can in some cases facilitate a major breakthrough which would otherwise have taken months or even years of less intensive therapy. Regardless of its significance in facilitating movement, rage and anger work is at the most only a part of the overall therapeutic process. In Troy's case, it was the beginning of a long involved recovery from childhood trauma.

After his rage work, Troy was overcome with guilt. I had seen this happen many times before. The intensity of his rage and hatred for his father was more than he could live with at that time, so he retreated into a familiar emotional position of self-loathing and guilt. He was miserable, but at least he was familiar with this particular kind of misery.

Familiar misery is only comfortable for a short period of time if the person has known something better. Troy had a taste of the empowerment of claiming his worth and value with all of his physical and emotional strength while doing anger work. He had liked it. Because of this, Troy did some more anger work after a few days. Each time he did this, he moved further out of the rage and more into healthy anger and empowerment. His statements while hitting the mat changed from "Stop it!" and "Get off me!" to "It was wrong!" and finally, "I'm a good person!" and "My body is good." When I see sexual abuse victims hitting the mat or pillow with all their physical and emotional strength while making positive statements about themselves, I know significant progress has been made. What starts as rage and hatred transforms into love of self and enforcement of appropriate emotional boundaries for self-protection.

WHEN RAGE BECOMES ADDICTIVE

The powerful rush of adrenaline that often accompanies anger feels good. It actually gives a person greater physical strength temporarily while the adrenaline is being released (as with Joyce and the Chevy in Chapter 1). After the release of anger, there is often a sense of euphoria and general well-being. If there has been a significant physical exertion during the expression of anger, there may also be endorphins released into the bloodstream, creating an even greater feeling of pleasure. All of this adds up to one point: we can get addicted to explosive releases of anger and rage.

It feels bad to store up feelings. We get tense, irritable and uneasy. We may even develop physical pain from the tension, and possibly develop stress-related illnesses. The relief from tension experienced during aggressive behavior actually creates good feelings on a physical level, although we may be in great pain emotionally. That's the nature of addiction. When pleasant feelings become associated with unhealthy and destructive behavior, we get addicted to that behavior, as in the cases of Joe and Cora described previously.

The diagram of the addictive cycle in Figure 4.2 helps to illustrate how the pattern of suppression and explosion develops. The cycle begins when our needs for love, nurturance, support and security go unmet in childhood. This includes experiences of neglect, abandonment, rejection and the many types of direct abuse. Part of being born as a vulnerable child in an imperfect world means having experiences that are painful and frightening. As illustrated in Figure 4.2, one of the ways we protect ourselves from more pain is through the use of anger.

Our parents were not educated about the healthy value of anger as an emotion, so they usually punished or rejected us when we displayed this emotion. If you follow the cycle illustrated in Figure 4.2, you will see how this leads to anger suppression and shame. Unfortunately, we continue to be hurt in various ways, and many of our needs continue to go unmet. This causes a build-up of anger and frustration, leading to a breaking point in a situation we feel is "safe" to release our anger. The problem is that we tend to feel the safest (and the most angry) in our homes with those we love. This is also where we tend to have experiences of feeling "that's the last straw!"

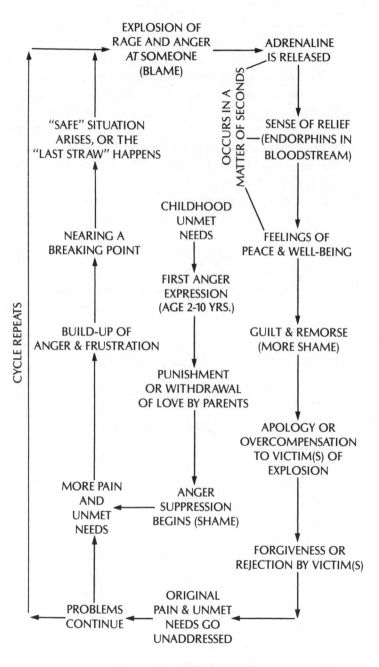

EXPLOSION OF
RAGE AND ANGER
AT SOMEONE
(BLAME)

ADRENALINE
IS RELEASED

OCCURS IN A
MATTER OF SECONDS

"SAFE" SITUATION
ARISES, OR THE
"LAST STRAW" HAPPENS

SENSE OF RELIEF
(ENDORPHINS IN
BLOODSTREAM)

CHILDHOOD
UNMET
NEEDS

NEARING A
BREAKING POINT

FEELINGS OF
PEACE & WELL-BEING

FIRST ANGER
EXPRESSION
(AGE 2-10 YRS.)

CYCLE REPEATS

BUILD-UP OF
ANGER & FRUSTRATION

GUILT & REMORSE
(MORE SHAME)

PUNISHMENT
OR WITHDRAWAL
OF LOVE BY PARENTS

APOLOGY OR
OVERCOMPENSATION
TO VICTIM(S) OF
EXPLOSION

MORE PAIN
AND
UNMET
NEEDS

ANGER
SUPPRESSION
BEGINS (SHAME)

FORGIVENESS OR
REJECTION BY VICTIM(S)

PROBLEMS
CONTINUE

ORIGINAL
PAIN & UNMET
NEEDS GO
UNADDRESSED

Figure 4.2. Addictive Cycle

This is when the explosion occurs, and we have that rush of power and energy. At this point in the cycle, we may be verbally, emotionally or physically abusive. This usually leads to an apology or an attempt to "make it up to" the person or persons we have hurt. Some people don't do this part; they just retreat into tremendous shame and guilt and don't say a word about what has happened. Some powerful denial and blocking can occur at this point if the person is incapable of processing what has actually happened.

When apology or compensation does occur, the victim(s) may or may not forgive the abuser. It really does not matter. If the shame goes unhealed, the forgiveness will not be accepted. What matters is whether or not the person in the addictive cycle takes care of unfinished business from the past. If they do, they've broken the cycle. If not, they will repeat the cycle and there will be more pain and suffering for all concerned. The following chapters are designed to provide as many healthy ways as possible to break this cycle of rage and anger addiction.

THE SLOW LEAK OF SEETHING RAGE

Verna's face looked as if it hadn't broken into a smile in a long time, if ever. As a matter of fact, she looked as if her face would break if she even tried to smile. Her mouth was pinched so tight, she had just about eliminated her lips. She looked angry, all right, but even more than that, she looked incredibly sad.

When she began telling me her life story, I realized this woman did not know how she came across. She didn't know she had rage inside and she didn't know how sad she looked. What she felt and how she looked was normal to her. It was all she had ever known. She had no basis for comparison.

When her uncle molested her as a child, she thought that was something all uncles did to their nieces. She had no comparative life experience to tell her otherwise. She only came to counseling because she was having a hard time controlling her anger.

Verna's seething rage made her hard to look at. Like Sam in the first chapter, her eyes looked accusing and even vicious. Also, like Sam, her words told nothing of the rage and sadness in her face and eyes.

Sexual abuse had run rampant throughout Verna's entire family. There was almost no one in her family who was not a victim, a perpetrator or both. A woman in her sixties, she had only begun to realize the extent of sexual abuse in her family in the past year. She had been living with rage all her life without even knowing it.

Verna's unexpressed, slowly-leaking rage had shaped her face, her body and her life. She had no close friends. The one relationship she did have, with her ex-husband, was a mutually abusive one. She was extremely miserable and for much of her life she didn't even know it.

Rage is poison. It either stays in and makes the person sick, or it is released in uncontrollable explosions and hurts others. Usually suppressed rage has many victims. This was the case with Verna, but she herself was the biggest victim of all.

Verna was so sick from the seething and its consequences (love deprivation, mainly) that she didn't have the strength to physically release her 60 years of rage. When it came her turn in group to try anger work, she was willing, but she just couldn't hit the pillow hard enough to express what she felt. Verna's release was to come in another way.

After some Gestalt work to clarify that her core being was the good person she knew herself to be, I had her get into a fetal position on the mat. She did so without question, which surprised me. I then had all the other group members gather around Verna and put their hands on her and push. I instructed Verna to push against the hands, as if they represented her cold hard shell and she was the good innocent being within. I told the group members to push back and not allow her to move. Her comment after a few moments was, "This feels familiar."

Then I had the group members change their touch to
one of love, caressing and holding Verna's back, shoulders
and arms. Her words after a brief period were, "I'm staying right here." We accompanied this nurturing with affirmations like, "You're one of a kind, Verna. We're glad
you're here. It's safe to come out now. We like you just the
way you are." Verna soon raised up with a big childlike
smile. She didn't have to say a word. We knew she had
received the love and support we had offered. We all returned to our seats, and we went on to work with another
group member.

In only a few moments, Verna's smile had faded. The
old familiar look returned and she became silent. She cried
silently throughout the remainder of the group, grieving
over the losses of the precious child she had just discovered. She smiled again, however, when each group member
gave her feedback on the work she had done, telling their
feelings upon seeing her smile for the first time as she
rose up from her childlike position on the mat. Her healing
had begun. By finding her inner child, she had discovered
a reason to go through the long and arduous process of
recovery. She knew where she was going, and she had
already tasted drops of the sweetness that awaited her
when she would begin to give and receive love.

Perhaps the most destructive rage we have known on
this planet was that of Adolf Hitler. I understand that he
was abused horribly as a child and raised by rigidly compulsive and controlling parents. This does not in any way
excuse what he did. It is merely to point out the extensive
destruction which can result from suppressed and seething rage, when it is released in a systematic and mecha-
nized manner. Murder and rape are both forms of uncontrolled rage we are familiar with. Many times when I
have seen big, strong men pounding the mat, I have had
the profound feeling that lives were being saved or rapes
were being prevented. The rage has to go somewhere and
mats and pillows are safe recipients for it. When people
are its victims, the results are devastating.

Unlike Hitler, Verna did the necessary work to start her recovery. She is getting well. At 61, she is committed to making her life work. Her rage is being transformed in therapy into manageable emotions related to resolvable issues. Yes, rage is frightening, but only when it is left unaddressed and unresolved.

Clean out your refrigerator and throw out the old moldy vegetables. Clear out your emotions and work through the old unexpressed pain, fear and anger from your past. If you have already done that, then go around being happy and expressing all of your emotions while they are fresh. You will set a great example just by taking care of yourself in front of others.

The best thing I can do for the world is to take care of myself.

My emotions are my responsibility.

When I blame another for a feeling I am having, I am giving my power to that person and declaring myself a victim.

Expressing my feelings is as important for my health as eating, sleeping and breathing.

5

Becoming Intimate
With Anger

Have you ever been afraid of really loving someone? Have you been afraid of letting someone really love you? Most of us have known this fear. To love and be loved is what we want more than anything, so why would we be so afraid of having the deep, intimate experience of loving and being loved?

Why is it that domestic violence is considered by the police to be the most dangerous situation they can walk into? Why do we feel the most fear and anger with those we love the most? These are important questions. Let's consider some possible answers.

We have never been more vulnerable and susceptible to pain than we were as children. The deepest pain and greatest fear for many of us occurred in our childhood. The most painful adult experiences we have are those which in some way connect with our childhood losses and injuries. Look at the circles in Figure 5.1. The primary emotional experience we have is the need for love. Because this need is never perfectly met, we are hurt. Because we are hurt, we learn to fear. When we are afraid, we defend ourselves — often with anger.

Figure 5.1. Outer Circle

As adults, we "fall" in love. This experience of loving at some point reminds us of how we were hurt in past experiences of loving. Of course, we are afraid of being hurt, no matter how big, strong or healthy we may happen to be. So we try to protect ourselves. This is human nature.

It follows that the more we love, the more potential we have to be hurt, afraid and angry. Fortunately the love can grow and mature in such a way that the pain and fear are minimized and we no longer need anger for protection from those we love. This happens as our skill, strength, knowledge and awareness expand, allowing the more vulnerable inner core of love to grow and expand into the world around us. You can imagine this by picturing the walls of protection, fear and pain breaking down, allowing the inner circle of love in Figure 5.1 to expand and blend with the outer circle of skill, strength, knowledge and awareness. So how does this happen in real life?

THE FIRST STEP TO TRUE INTIMACY

The first step to true intimacy is to know, understand and become intimate with yourself. Your self is what you bring into a relationship. If you don't know this self or you feel ashamed of some part it, you will not be able or willing to share those aspects with your loved one. If there are wounds that have not healed, you will automatically hide and protect those wounded parts. You will not offer yourself fully to another, as is required for true intimacy, unless you feel good about the self you are offering.

This simply means that each of us must make a journey into ourselves to learn about our own defense mechanisms, to manage our fear and to heal our pain. Only then can we reach the healing core of love that is the heart of who we are. Only then will we be willing to allow someone else to really know and love us for all that we are.

In Figure 5.1 you'll notice a new ring has been added to the concentric circles. That is what we face the world with. When we meet someone, we don't immediately say, "Hi! I'd like to tell you about my feelings. I'm hurt, afraid and angry and I need a lot of love." The first part of ourselves we offer to others is what we consider to be our best self. We smile, shake hands or hug and act as if everything is just fine, whether it is or not. We show our social skills, demonstrate our knowledge and awareness in our conversation and try to give the impression of being a healthy, together person. This is the realm in which we operate at work or with people we don't know very well. This is the part of ourselves we use to "make a good impression" on someone we like. This may even be all we really know of ourselves.

In school and throughout our lives, we have gained knowledge, skill, strength and awareness about the world around us. We never had a course on how to experience, understand and express our emotions, although it would have been a good idea. No one told us that our anger was okay or that it is normal to feel hurt and afraid. It's time now to begin to learn inner strength, self-knowledge, self-awareness and skills for dealing with our emotions. In other words, it's time to learn to accept, experience and express all of our emotions in healthy ways, regardless of what they may be.

In Figure 5.2 you will see two diagrams, one with the arrows pointing out into the world, and one with the arrows pointing into the inner world. In the first diagram the focus is on knowledge about the world we see with our eyes and hear about with our ears. In the second diagram the focus is on the inner world, and our eyes and ears can't tell us about what's going on in there. We have to learn new ways of seeing and listening to learn about the world within. Chapters Six and Nine will give you some ideas about how you may be able to see and hear more clearly what is going on inside yourself.

WHAT ARE YOUR FAVORITE DEFENSES?

As indicated in the diagrams of concentric circles, we tend to protect and defend ourselves by withdrawing, getting angry or some combination of the two. A good first step to take on the journey within is to identify your own defense mechanisms.

Maybe you never get angry. On the other hand, you may feel angry all the time. Do you know how to take a break in a relationship to give yourself time to think and calm down? Are you always pulling away until you explode in anger? Don't judge yourself at this point, just figure out how you protect yourself.

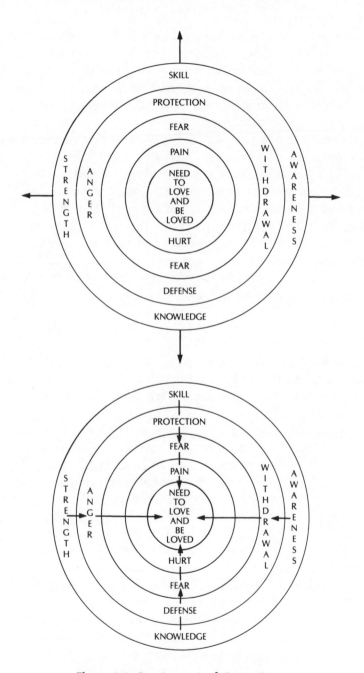

Figure 5.2. Our Inner And Outer Focus

Next ask yourself what you are afraid of when you are using these defense methods. We are usually afraid of being hurt, either through direct abuse or some form of rejection or abandonment. Notice that the two basic types of anger correspond to the two basic types of fear. We protect ourselves through anger and withdrawal, and we are afraid of being abused (unhealthy expressions of anger directed at us) or rejected (withdrawal of love).

Next comes the hardest part. Facing our pain and experiencing it completely through to a point of resolution is one of the most frightening and difficult parts of becoming intimate with ourselves. Our pain falls into the same two basic categories as our fears and defenses. Our deepest pain came when we were abused, abandoned or both.

So this is the journey. You're probably saying to yourself, "Great. So how do I do it?"

BREAKING THROUGH THE WALLS OF FEAR

Expressing anger in healthy, safe ways provides the strength needed to break through the walls of fear and resolve the pain, allowing the free, healthy expression of love.

Remember Paul, the man who couldn't connect with his wife and son? His story provides an excellent example of anger as an important part of breaking through the walls of fear, allowing more open expression of other emotions in intimate family relationships. After his anger work, in conjunction with the Gestalt release and inner-child integration, Paul was able to connect meaningfully with his son and begin a new dimension of intimacy in his marriage.

James's journey within was a much more difficult one. At 37, he had never been married and had only been romantically involved with one woman for a very short period of time. When I first saw him, he had been using cocaine and marijuana heavily and was completely isolated from relationships of any kind. James was employed as a computer programmer. His work was his only involvement with the world around him. It would be accurate to say that he had absolutely no intimacy in his life at all.

Both of James's parents were dead and he only communicated with one of his sisters. His father had been an alcoholic and rageaholic who had abused everyone in the family. James had been very close to his mother, who took it upon herself to protect him from his father's abuse.

"I've always been afraid. I don't remember a time when I was not afraid." James had a blank look on his face as he talked. He was a nice-looking man, slim and well dressed.

"I just remember feeling like I was hiding behind my mother from my dad the whole time I was growing up. He was always yelling about something. Mom had always been my best friend. I don't know what I would have done without her." James started to cry at this point, and I could tell how much grief he had yet to face over his mother's death.

For weeks James showed no progress in therapy. While doing family-of-origin work one afternoon, he agreed to try some anger work. He had been reluctant to do this, stating "I hate anger. I'm afraid I'll be just like him." He was referring, of course, to his father. He was paralyzed by his fear, and yet the very emotion that could help him claim his power was detestable to him. After only a few seconds of hitting the mat, he stopped and grabbed his head with both hands.

"What are you feeling?" I asked.

"I'm afraid," was his reply. His anger had taken him deeper into his fear and he had not been able to break through. His isolation continued, dictated by the fear that said very clearly, "To trust others means to be hurt."

James had no feeling of power or control in his life. His fear had control of him. Without the empowerment of anger, he was indeed paralyzed. His determination to be the opposite of his father added to his dilemma. I knew he would have to get angry, and that it was only a matter of time.

The first sign that he was getting ready came when I saw him starting to smile and laugh more. I reasoned that the more he enjoyed his life, the more likely he was to claim his power to get well and overcome his fear. I asked if he was ready to try some more anger work.

"I'm ready to do something! I'm sick of being scared all the time." He was showing more emotional energy than I had seen before.

"Just strike out against that wall of fear," I coached him as he knelt on the mat, staring at the pillow. "See if you can break through." He broke through, all right. He raged long and hard, ending up with a winded smile on his face.

"That felt good," he said between gasps for air. I then suggested he go inside himself, find that scared little boy and offer him some of the strength he was feeling. I guided him through a visualization designed to allow him to embrace his frightened inner child, offering self-nurturing to replace the lost love and support of his mother. I really felt good about this session. I had no idea what was coming next.

James went into a rage that lasted a week. He didn't hurt anyone, but he griped, cursed and complained at anyone who was anything less than perfect. On a Friday afternoon at the end of a long day, I was listening to his complaints about the imperfections of the world. I gradually talked him down and he became quiet. He had some legitimate concerns, and my support of these seemed to calm him. No sooner did he calm down then he began to sob deeply.

As a therapist, I have witnessed a lot of crying. I had never seen anything like I saw James go through that day. He cried nonstop for over an hour. Deep, body-shaking sobs gripped and shook him. I didn't know anyone could cry that deeply for that long. Afterward, he was exhausted for days.

Then a new James began to emerge. He had broken through the wall of fear, grieved the pain and reconnected with his love. He had used his skill, strength and knowledge to make the journey into himself. Now he was ready to start learning how to risk and reach out in relationships with others.

NO ANGER, NO BOUNDARIES, NO INTIMACY

Anger is an important part of a healthy boundary system. It provides the firm and powerful feeling needed to create an experience of safety and comfort within. Without skills for expressing anger in healthy ways, effective boundaries are impossible. Without effective boundaries and the accompanying feelings of security, vulnerability is too frightening and intimacy is out of the question.

When it is expressed in healthy ways, anger may not even look like anger. If anger were always aggressive, as we often expect, it would not be at all helpful in creating intimacy. Here are some points to consider about anger, when it is expressed in healthy ways:

- Healthy, current anger involves no blame or accusing.
- When expressed in appropriate ways, anger is nothing more than focused and directed emotional energy.
- When focused and directed, emotional energy gives emphasis, strength and clarity to expression.
- Healthy anger does not attack or hurt anyone.
- Healthy anger is an expression of love.

As an expression of love, healthy anger gives strength to personal boundaries. Without the empowerment of anger, boundaries are too soft and in some cases, nonexistent. When expressed appropriately, anger gives us the security we need to risk the vulnerability of true intimacy.

BUILDING HEALTHY BOUNDARIES

When we are clear and focused within ourselves, boundaries automatically emerge and begin to move into place. In other words, boundaries are to some extent established subconsciously, as a result of mature self-love. (This will be explored further in Chapter 11.) Another dimension of boundaries requires our consciously focused attention and effort. We will look at these two levels in terms of our commitment to ourselves and to our relationships.

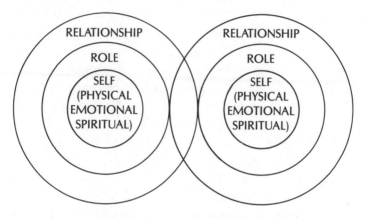

Figure 5.3. Commitment Priorities

In Figure 5.3 you will see a graphic representation of commitment priorities in relationships, which seem to be necessary for stability, clarity and intimacy. The inner circle represents commitment to self, the next ring represents the role we play in the relationship and the outer ring represents our commitment to the relationship itself. You will notice there is no mention of commitment to the other person — that's their job.

1. COMMITMENT TO SELF

Our first priority in a relationship with another is our commitment to ourselves. This is not selfish, it's merely practical.

Your best friend has just been in a car wreck and needs your help. You want to get there as fast as you can, but it's a few miles away and your car's gas tank is on empty. Do you ignore this and zoom off to the rescue? Of course not. You get some gas before making the trip. By the same token, we each need to take care of our own needs to some extent before we go about trying to give to others.

It's really very simple. You are the center of your universe. Everything you see, hear, feel and experience goes out in concentric spheres from your point of awareness there in the center of your world. This is not some weird idea, it's pure rational fact.

You are on top of your world, as I am on top of mine. The planet is round. Each of us is sticking off the side of it, pulled toward its center by gravity. There really is no top or bottom to this planet, but we think in terms of top and bottom, up and down, for the purpose of communication. So it seems helpful to say we are each on top of our own world to further illustrate the point that each of us is at the center of our own universe. No one can push you off the top of your world. The top of your world is wherever you are. Wherever you go, there you are — on top of your world. That's why it makes such practical sense that your first priority of commitment be to yourself.

Your self, your universe as you perceive it, is what you carry into any relationship you enter. You are responsible for what you contribute to the relationship. The other person is responsible for their own contribution. This means simply that you have the job of maintaining your own physical, emotional, mental and spiritual health. That way you bring a healthy person into the relationship, which is a true gift to your partner.

Let's look at some of the inner dimensions to your relationship with yourself. Figure 5.4 gives some ideas for what our priorities within ourselves might be. The physical self is closer to the surface and more observable than any of the other aspects. We share our thoughts and ideas more easily and readily than we do our emotions, so the mental self would be next.

Our emotional self goes very deep into our being and much of it is subconscious. Our emotions are more private than many of our thoughts, so we may see them as closer to the core of our being. Within the emotional self we find the anger, fear, pain and love that was depicted in earlier diagrams.

You might say that the spiritual self or the spiritual aspects of love are at the heart of who we are. Our spiritual feelings, experiences and beliefs are deeper and more private than perhaps any other aspect of who we are. The spiritual dimension naturally expands to include the emotional, mental and physical self as focus and development occur at this deepest level of relationship.

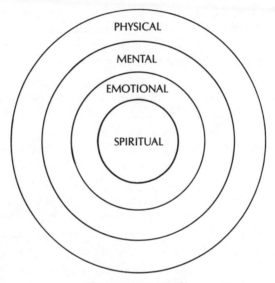

Figure 5.4. Your Self

This is our first work in creating a healthy relationship with another. It takes two basically healthy, growing people to make a healthy relationship.

2. COMMITMENT TO ROLE

We are each responsible for the role we play in our relationships. It is a mistake to make our role totally dependent on the behavior of the other. For example, "I would be a better husband if she would only . . . I am responsible for the kind of husband or wife I am, no matter what my spouse may or may not do. My role is my creation."

By taking charge of defining your role as husband, wife, lover, friend, mother, father, son, daughter, boss or employee, you are empowering yourself in the relationship and removing yourself from the victim position. The tricky part about this is that our basic training for these roles was in our family of origin and early childhood experience. This is one of the reasons that family-of-origin work is so important as a part of any treatment or recovery program.

Here are some ideas to help you clarify and take charge of the roles you play in your significant relationships:

1. Write down what you learned about the roles of wife and mother from your mother, and husband and father roles from your father. (Add any other roles you are interested in exploring, the source being your primary role model in that area.) This will give you an idea of your subconscious mind-set regarding these roles.

2. Write new definitions of these roles for yourself, using your own knowledge and goals as guidelines.

3. Next write about all the reasons you feel you cannot fulfill the ideal roles you have defined for yourself. Identify whether you are blaming anyone else — that is, whether you are in a victim position. Acknowledge this, and if possible, let it go.

4. Create affirmations in first person, present tense to form new attitudes and beliefs about yourself and your ability to fulfill your own ideal role in your relationships.

5. Plan specific behaviors that will help you to actualize your ideal role fulfillment.

This is a further extension of what you offer in your relationship. Your commitment is to bring into the relationship a healthy, growing individual who is further committed to being the best spouse, lover, parent or friend possible. All of this happens before even considering the influence of the other person.

3. COMMITMENT TO THE RELATIONSHIP

This is where we really begin to give consideration to the thoughts, feelings and needs of the other person. You will notice in Figure 5.3 that the outer ring marked "relationship" is the only part of the two circles that overlap. This is to indicate we each have individual responsibility for ourselves and our roles, and we share mutual responsibility for our relationships. When our commitment follows this priority, we bring a healthy person with well-defined functional roles into the relationship. Therefore, our contribution to the relationship is the best we have to offer and we are responsible for our contribution.

There is a tremendous amount of material that could be covered under the heading of boundaries and this covers only a small part of that subject matter. In Chapter 11, "Expanding The Circle From Within," boundaries will be explored further, particulary in the discussion of Figure 11.4. The point here is that emotional, mental, physical and spiritual health automatically create a powerful basis for functional boundaries. In making your health your responsibility and your first priority of commitment in your relationship, you are making an important step in creating healthy boundaries.

With these steps taken, we are ready to invest all that we choose in our relationship, making intimacy a possibility. If we do not claim our anger as part of who we are, we will be rejecting part of ourselves, which is unhealthy and can create illness and dis-ease. Without at some point claiming our anger and its sense of empowerment, we do not feel the strength and courage necessary to risk true intimacy, sharing our deepest feelings, thoughts and dreams. Without healthy anger, we certainly will not have healthy boundaries.

THE WONDERS OF TRUE INTIMACY

There is no greater intimacy than that which we knew with our mothers while in the warm, peaceful silence of the womb. Since the moment of birth, when we were separated physically from that warm safety, we have been constantly seeking some way to recreate that experience of peaceful bliss with feelings of comfort and security.

This is one of the reasons that we want to be intimate as adults, no matter how frightening or unfamiliar it may feel. To be wrapped in the love of the one we trust, physically and emotionally open to giving and receiving, is the closest we come to recreating that total bliss of the first few months of life.

To many, the term intimacy means sexual involvement. One of the reasons sexual contact is so important is that it sometimes creates many of the same feelings of physical warmth that we felt in the womb. As we all know, however, sexual involvement without commitment and a feeling of safety leads to the opposite of comfort and security. This is why we need our priorities of commitment intact and need to be friends with our anger before risking sexual or other types of intimate involvement.

True healthy intimacy does not come easily. The journey is long and challenging with many pitfalls. We keep trying because it offers one of the highest levels of human experience possible. There is a miraculous healing expansion of love that spontaneously occurs when we open our hearts to one another. The rewards of intimacy are so great and enticing that we sometimes get them mixed up with a mystical or spiritual experience. We can even get caught up in a process of idolizing our loved one, expecting them to solve all our problems and make our lives forever wonderful. This leads to the heartbreak of co-dependency and love addiction, and ultimately to disillusionment and isolation.

The wonders of true intimacy can only be experienced when we have established a deep level of intimacy with ourselves, claiming and expressing all of our emotions openly and honestly.

I am developing skills for maintaining my safety while being vulnerable in relationships.

The more I care for myself, the more I have to offer to others.

Intimacy begins with the journey into myself.

The journey into myself is as vast and unlimited as the journey into the world around me.

The more I trust myself, the more I can trust those around me.

6

Protecting The Child Within

Mature adult anger is not a childlike emotion. It is specifically for the protection and safety of the vulnerable inner self or the child within. When anger is expressed in a childlike manner, it provides no safety but simply causes more problems. Because we were not provided with healthy role models for mature emotional expression, many of us still express our emotions in childlike ways. Another way of saying this is that until we have healed and resolved issues from our past, our emotional self remains stuck in our childhood.

Childlike anger blames and accuses, taking no responsibility. Mature anger is an expression of personal power and takes total responsibility. Mature anger is specifically for the purpose of keeping the vulnerable inner child safe and secure. Take a look at Figure 6.1.

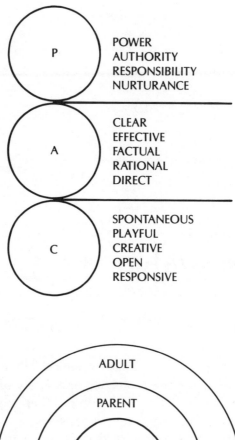

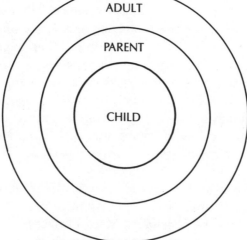

Figure 6.1. Two Views of P-A-C

You can see in the first diagram that the words "Power" and "Authority" go in the realm of the inner parent. These are words that go with the expression of mature, healthy anger. The inner child is associated with the more vulnerable emotions of fear, pain and the need for love, represented by the inner three circles in Figure 5.1. All of the emotions of the inner child can be expressed in mature adult ways. The point here is to identify the protective nature of anger and its rightful place in the realm of the inner parent. You can also see that the relationship between the inner child and the inner parent goes right through the adult self. Our behavior as adults is thus a reflection of our internal relationship with ourselves.

The second diagram in Figure 6.1 shows another perspective on the parent, adult and child. The adult is on the outer layer, because that is what we greet the world with. The inner parent comes next, because it is the buffer between the world and the inner child. The inner child is the deepest aspect of our being, where our emotional and spiritual self resides. All of this is communicated with the world through the adult as the diagram indicates. Anything coming from the inner child will be filtered through the inner parent and the adult before reaching the world outside. If as adults we lose control, the childlike emotion explodes through the inner parent and supersedes the adult. This is when we might say the child has "taken over."

This is analogous to the diagram in Figure 5.1. The adult is the outer ring of Figure 5.1, the realm of skill, strength, knowledge and awarenesss. The parent is next, the ring of protection that contains anger and withdrawal. The child is represented by all three of the inner circles, containing the vulnerable feelings of fear, pain and the need for love, which includes the capacity for joy.

THE SOFT VULNERABLE INNER CHILD

Many of us, particularly men, cringe at the thought of being soft and vulnerable. That's one reason there is so

much effort put into creating that tough, hard exterior
— just to make sure no one suspects there are fear, pain
and a need for love underneath. It's a sure bet that the
tougher and meaner the exterior, the deeper the wounds
of the inner child.

We all entered the world wide open, totally vulnerable.
We have found that there is no such thing as forgetting,
that unneeded or painful memories are only blocked from
conscious memory so we can move forward and continue
to function. This means subconsciously each of us remembers that experience of being totally open and vulnerable. We knew the greatest love and the greatest pain
in that stage of our existence. This is why it is safe to say
that within each of us is a soft vulnerable self, however
deeply it may be buried in the subconscious mind.

Most of us have seen the tattoo on the muscular, hairy
arm of a tough-looking man that says simply, "Mother."
To me this is the man's connection with his own inner
softness, which was experienced most profoundly when
he was a child with his mother. I have worked with many
big strong angry men, some of whom were abusers. Within each of them we discovered a frightened, wounded
child, open and vulnerable and in great need of love.

I have talked about a certain type of man to make the
point of the universal existence of inner softness because
the vulnerability of many others is easy to see. Some of
us, male and female, show our inner feelings whether we
like it or not. We may have never learned to hide them.
This can be both a blessing and a curse, depending on
what the feelings are and when and where we show them.

To be vulnerable does not mean to be weak. We can
learn to share our deep intimate feelings in a very open
manner while exercising sophisticated skills for taking
care of ourselves. The fact is that we are all emotionally
vulnerable at our core. That's not a problem. It is in fact
a blessing. By sharing our vulnerability with each other,
we provide the opportunity to lay down the defenses we
have always used to protect and distance ourselves. To

approach someone with our heart and both hands open and exposed indicates there is no threat. We can trust. It is safe.

I invite you to make the journey into yourself and see if you can find your own inner child, the most vulnerable aspect of your being. The rewards for the discovery are virtually without limit. To fully experience your emotions is to be completely involved in life. To deny your inner emotional self is to live a half-way existence of boredom, fear and internal conflict.

I JUST CAN'T FEEL ANYTHING

Lora first approached me following a brief talk I had given on anger management. She was a very attractive woman in her late thirties who presented herself in a pleasant confident manner. I was surprised at the casual way in which she spoke her first words to me.

"I was an incest victim of my father and brother, and I have been raped five times. I think I'm doing fine, but I seem to be angry at my daughter and husband a lot. Do you think I need to come see you?" I love it when people do that. They want me to play the doctor role and tell them what to do.

"Do you want to come see me?" I smiled as I turned her question back to her. She knew what I was doing and smiled back. "Yes."

I don't usually do this so early in a counseling relationship, but I felt compelled to tell her what I was thinking.

"I want to be very honest with you about something. With the kind of history you have, you may not be able to let go and experience your emotions the way you need to in an outpatient setting. I want you to consider inpatient treatment, so you will have 24-hour care and support while you are working through the deeper and more intense emotions."

I knew before I was through talking that she wasn't ready for that. She took one of my cards and said she would give me a call to set up an appointment.

During her therapy sessions in the coming weeks, Lora talked openly about her history of abuse and about her adult life. Never a tear was shed. I saw no sign of emotion in her whatsoever. She was even calm and objective while describing an incident when her father had physically hurt her while molesting her. I knew she would have to tell these stories many times before she started to feel. I signed her up for an intensive Focus group in my office, in hopes that the concentrated work might help her get in touch with her feelings.

Lora went through all the motions without any of the emotions. She stated that she felt no connection at all with her inner child. In her inner-child work, she was so detached from the experience that I discontinued the exercise. The only thing that seemed to touch her was Gestalt work with her daughter. She admitted to verbally and physically abusing her throughout childhood and adolescence. This was where she was stuck. Her guilt for the abuse to her daughter would not allow her to feel compassion for herself. She felt as if she did not deserve to grieve for her own losses since she had inflicted so much pain on her own child.

After the intensive group, Lora asked to go into the hospital. She knew she was not going to get what she needed on an outpatient basis. For the first four weeks in the hospital, her defenses remained intact. I heard her say, "I still don't feel anything" so many times that it became a joke. She was great at helping the other patients, but she just could not seem to help herself. It was the sessions with her daughter that really started the ball rolling.

"Susan, I've been in the hospital almost four weeks now, and I'm not making any progress. I feel so guilty about abusing you that I won't allow myself to do what I need to do to get well. I'm only telling you this because my therapist suggested it, and I don't know what else to do." Lora shed a few tears as she spoke to her daughter but I could see she was very much on guard.

The word "forgiveness" was not spoken in the sessions with her daughter, but that is exactly what happened.

"Mom, I want you to get well. I want you to come home." At 14, Susan was not able to talk about all of her feelings, but she got her point across. She obviously had a lot of emotional problems of her own because of the abuse she had received. She wanted her mom to get well so the abuse would stop. She wanted her mom home because she was the only mom she had and her stepfather just couldn't take her place. The innocence and simplicity of Susan's words set her mother free to move in her therapy.

When Lora started to experience her emotions, it was something to behold. Her normal expression was a somewhat stoic "I've got it all together" look. The first time she really cried in therapy, it was as if her mask broke and a childlike whimper took over her entire face. It only lasted for a few seconds before she got it under control and the mask was back in place. Her wounded inner child had peeked through, and I saw and heard what seemed like a three- or four-year-old's expression of pain and fear. Her emotions were stuck way back in her childhood. Letting them surface was a terrifying experience for the adult Lora.

Prior to this her only emotional expression had been anger, and it had also been childlike. When angry, Lora blamed and attacked whoever was nearest. This is what many of us think anger is. That's because mature adult anger is rare, and when it is expressed, it often doesn't even seem like anger at all.

Ordinarily Lora's voice was fairly deep and somewhat nasal. When she began doing anger work, her voice was a high-pitched infantile squeal. As she continued to progress, her emotional voice deepened and matured, until she was able to express her anger at the abuse that was perpetrated on her with a powerful adult woman's expression of rage and indignation. She was connecting with her inner child, bringing her emotional self out of the past and into the present to become a significant part of her life.

THE SOFT INNER EDGES OF ANGER

When I feel a client is ready, I move them immediately into self-nurturing after an explosion of rage and anger in therapy. The explosion comes from a recognition that what happened to them was wrong and that they deserved to be treated with love and respect. The outer explosion is strong and abrasive, but the inner strength comes from the need for love and protection. When Lora first expressed rage at her father for abusing her, she cried deeply. I knew it was time for her to turn the strength of her anger into self-nurturing protection and love.

"Did you feel your strength when you were hitting the mat?" I was talking softly to Lora, sitting on the floor next to her, as she knelt on the edge of the mat.

She nodded, "Yes."

"Then take that strength to that little girl who was hurt by her father. Put your hand on his chest and slowly, steadily push him out of the room. Keep pushing him until he is gone. When he is completely out of the picture, go back to that little girl and pick her up. Wrap your strength and your love around her and tell her she's safe now, that you will protect her. Feel the power of your love for that innocent little girl. Give her what she needs. Be the parent to yourself that you always wanted and never had. Now take her into your heart, where she lives." I chose the words that seemed to fit, based on what I knew of Lora and her level of readiness. I was also sitting very close to her, sensing what she needed at each moment.

This is a standard part of rage and anger work as I use it in my practice. The procedure never stops with the explosive release. The power and strength of the anger is always translated into protection and ultimately love for the inner child. This is the soft inner edge of anger.

HOW DOES THIS WORK ON A DAILY BASIS?

Once the basic healing work is done, the next challenge facing us is how to take care of ourselves day by day outside a therapeutic environment. This requires the same kind of strength that was needed to break through the wall of fear and face the pain. Without a continued dedication to self-love and inner focus, we slip all too easily into old unhealthy patterns.

Remember the story of Joyce, the woman who lifted the car off her son? The same kind of power and strength is available to each of us when we love and care for our vulnerable inner child. Of course, we won't have occasion to lift a car off our inner child, but we will all continue to need tremendous inner strength to express our innermost feelings openly and to take care of our emotional needs.

Here are some suggestions for taking care of yourself and maintaining a connection with your inner child:

- Create space and time in your daily schedule to talk to and listen to your inner child. (There are many books and tapes available to help you with this process including information on parenting and your child's anger. You will find them listed under the headings "References" and "Audiocassettes" in the back of this book.)
- Make your quiet time alone just as important as your time for your spouse, for your children and for paying the bills.
- When your body is showing signs of stress, that's your inner child saying, "Slow down. You're not Superman or Superwoman, and you're neglecting me, your inner self."
- Systematically and consistently create opportunities to express your feelings openly in a safe environment. Find a support group or a group of friends, and get together regularly for the purpose of keeping the door to your heart open.
- Create opportunities for laughter and fun. If you don't know how to play, then learn. Now there are conferences and workshops on play and laughter. For more information on play workshops, call Renaissance Educational Associates at 303-679-4309.

- Temporarily or permanently end all relationships in which you are being abused. Seek help, and only consider re-entering the relationship if the abuser has been through long-term intensive therapy and you have personally seen significant progress. Even then, proceed cautiously — you have a beautiful innocent child to protect.
- Only risk and commit to relationships in which you are loved. You deserve love and without it, you will not live fully.
- Embrace all that you are. Do not reject any aspect of your being. If you have problems, get help. You can have the life you always wanted — but it's up to you to create it.

Doing these things consistently after a lifetime of co-dependent and unhealthy relationships is no small task. You will need all of your energy and all of your physical, mental, emotional and spiritual power to make it.

SPIRITUAL POWER

I believe that one of the main reasons for the effectiveness of the 12-Step recovery programs is their spiritual basis. Like physical, mental and emotional power, spiritual power comes from within us. What sets the spiritual realm apart is that it is by definition — or lack of definition — without limits. Spiritual power comes from all around as well as within us. This gives us the comfort of knowing we don't have to go it alone. But we do have to go it.

My experience, both personal and professional, tells me that the more I maximize my human energy, strength and responsibility, the more spiritual power is available in my life. Physical, emotional and spiritual energy are the same. I don't claim it, I witness it. I claim responsibility for my physical, mental and emotional well-being. This is similar to my inner parent's acceptance of responsibility for my inner child. I work hard to take care of myself in these areas, and it seems that spiritually derived healing, knowledge and strength follow naturally and easily as a result. This follows from the idea that the essence of the inner child is spiritual, as illustrated in the diagrams in Figures 5.4 and 6.1.

My job is to care for and maximize this gift of life that is so precious to me. The reward that seems to follow is a quietly powerful flow of spirit which enhances every aspect of my being and experience. The word I use for the source of this flow is God.

DIALOGUES WITH THE INNER CHILD

To get in touch with your inner child, remember how you looked at the age of three or four years and try to get a clear mental image of yourself at that age. A photograph may be helpful, if you have one.

This is not only the child you once were, but the child you have always been. This is your emotional self, totally innocent and vulnerable. This is who you are deep inside.

Your inner child will teach you about your emotions and your need for love. The child within you lives in your heart, the emotional center of your body. It is helpful for you to picture your child self outside your body in order to communicate, but you are actually never apart. There are two phases to the inner child relationship. The first is the healing of your wounded child of the past. The second stage, which lasts the rest of your life, is nurturing your inner child of the present.

This child is not all that you are, however. You are also an adult who has survived a lifetime of risks and hardships, growing and learning along the way (whether you accept this fact or not). You have a brilliant mind, which you have used only partially because of the limitations of your parenting and the world you have lived in. There is much more to you than you know. There always will be. This is the miracle of life, love and learning. If you are fortunate enough to have already recognized your greatness, you probably know that you are still not through.

The closer we come to knowing who we really are, the more we realize how much we have to learn.

As an adult and inner parent, try making the following statements to your inner child and see what happens:

"I've been the kind of parent to you that my parents were to me. I didn't know any better. Like them, I have abandoned and neglected you at times without meaning to. I've treated you as if you weren't even there because I really didn't know you were there. I thought that when I grew up, you just went away.

"I realize now that I have even been abusive to you at times. You are all of my feelings, and I have always thought some of those feelings were bad. So I tried to control you with substances (food, cigarettes, alcohol, drugs, medication, work, sex, love relationships), thinking I could make the feelings I didn't like go away. It didn't work. The feelings just got worse. I realize now that I hurt you, and I'm sorry. I am ready to change now and take care of you. I accept you just as you are, no matter what you are feeling. Your feelings are my feelings, because you are who I am inside."

Now become the inner child. Sit on the floor, curl up on the couch or assume any childlike posture that seems to fit what you are feeling. As the inner child, you are only feelings. You don't think or analyze, you just feel. Try responding to your inner parent with:

"I'm glad you are finally recognizing me. I've been waiting for this for a long time. I like what you are saying. It makes me feel better. I'm not completely ready to trust you yet. I need to see some action. I need to be able to count on you throughout each day. I am completely dependent on you. If you don't love and care for me, no one will. You are all I have.

"When I am hurting or afraid, just hold me and tell me you love me. That's all I ask. Don't try to talk me out of my feelings, that's just who I am. Just love me and tell me that you'll protect me no matter what. I need to be told that you love me often, not just when things go wrong. When I am happy, I need you to smile and laugh and do fun things. I come out through your smile and laughter and playfulness. I also come out when you are loving and creative. I have a lot to offer you, if you will create a safe and healthy life for me. There is more joy and love in me than you have ever known, waiting to come out. Love and joy is who I am, and I am who you are. I'm counting on you. Please remember me."

If you're ready, you might respond with something like:

"You can count on me. I won't forget you. I will make mistakes, but I will learn to avoid repeating them. I accept you just as you are, no matter what you are feeling. Your feelings are my feelings. I love you unconditionally. You are who I am inside. In loving you, I love myself."

If you have difficulty with this exercise, write about your experience. This may help you figure out what you need to work on to get closer to the experience of self-love.

Your inner child may be too wounded or frightened for you to connect at this time. The concept may still seem foreign to you. If you like the words in this dialogue and you want to feel their depth and meaning, don't give up. Hang in there, and this will work for you. It has worked for me, and I still use these methods both personally and professionally.

I was born innocent and open.
The innocent open child I once was is still alive and
*   awake inside me right now.*
My inner child is all of my emotions.
I accept myself, no matter what I am feeling.
All of my feelings are okay with me.
I have the strength, skill and knowledge necessary to
*   protect and care for my vulnerable inner child.*
I am an adult with a precious child inside.
I have everything I need.
I am whole and complete.

7

The Role Of Anger In The Grief Process

The only bad thing about grieving is getting stuck in it. As long as we are moving through it, the grief process is a healing experience in which we learn and grow in important ways. When we are stuck in the grief process, serious problems can result. Here are some indications that a person is stuck in grief:

- They have stopped talking about the loss, and they don't want anyone else to bring it up. The subject is taboo.
- They use statements like, "I've dealt with that already. It's over." They may look sad, angry or depressed while saying this.
- There is a lack of joy and fulfillment in their life. They don't smile or laugh much.

- Substance abuse may be a problem.
- For some, major illness or a series of minor illnesses may begin to occur.
- They will begin to show general symptoms of depression, such as excessive sleeping, insomnia, weight loss or gain or an extremely pessimistic attitude.
- Angry outbursts may begin to occur for no apparent reason.
- There could be an unwillingness to trust or risk in relationships.
- The person may lose their will to live and actually become suicidal.

As you can tell, these symptoms can be potentially life-threatening. Learning how to grieve our losses effectively is an essential part of being an emotionally healthy person. Our life may depend on it.

TOO MUCH, TOO SOON

When Ray was only 11, he was already being asked to save lives. His mother was a bedridden asthmatic and he was given the responsibility to care for her.

"Dad loved sports. He lived, breathed, ate and drank athletics of all kinds. My brothers were big, strong star football players. I was small and liked to read. It seemed only natural that I would be the one to stay home with Mom." Ray had a way of talking off into space, as if he were watching his own private movie. It was a very sad movie, filled with pain and unresolved grief.

"I learned how to give CPR when I was 12. I saved my mother's life three times. One time, the one that stands out the most, I was sure that I had lost her. All I could think about was that I had let Dad down. I wasn't athletic and that hurt him, and now I was about to fail at the one job I had been really good at — keeping his wife, my mother, alive.

"She was already blue when I got to her. I had only gone to the bathroom. I worked on her for 45 minutes before the paramedics arrived. She just barely made it, and no one knew what I had been through but me. I couldn't talk about it. The fear, shame and guilt were just too strong. Finally they put her in the hospital. I still felt it was my responsibility to be with her. One night she seemed to be resting well so I decided to go home. I had spent six straight nights in a chair by her bed. She died 30 minutes after I left.

"No one blamed me. They didn't have to. I knew it was my fault. It seemed to me that I had been born to keep my mother alive — and now I had failed. As soon as I was old enough, I started riding fire trucks and ambulances and became certified as a paramedic. I was driven to be the first to every emergency, to save as many lives as I could. It was the only way I knew to make up for what I had done to my mother and to my family."

Ray's face was dark with his own thoughts and visions. The movie he was watching was filled with death and dying. Through the negligence of the adults around him, he had just had too much, too soon in his young life.

At 37 Ray looked like an unhealthy man of 55. He was in the hospital for his fifth serious suicide attempt. He had been clinically dead from these attempts three times. The real clincher in his depression was the vocation he had chosen. He blamed himself for the deaths of all the car-wreck victims, burn victims and drowning victims he had been unable to save. The fact that he had been in-strumental in saving hundreds of lives made no difference to him — that was expected. This was the most serious case of unresolved grief I had ever seen in my professional career. The task of helping him to see his life realistically and forgive himself seemed gigantic to me. Like Ray, I had no choice but to try.

I wrote the following poem about a female client with serious depression and rage problems. She was a lot like Ray. One of her suicide attempts had left her in a coma for three days. She came to me to deal with her anger.

Faith Eater

Dark and low she growls through life
Eating the ashes of her birth
Munching on morsels of meaning
Devouring all traces of worth

Eyes dark from cinders
Her vision burning with hate
She snarls at glimmers of goodness
Tearing and chewing at fate

From behind black eyes she mumbles her tale
Of frustrated struggles with death
She's come to me for sustenance
Ready to consume my breath

But I blow no winds of wisdom
I breathe no fragments of faith
Standing still in the ashes beside her
I see too clearly the wraith

Shocked, she shudders to notice
She's alone no more in her plight
Slowly we move through the wasteland
As I secretly search for the light

As her mind wanders, I see it
A spark, alive, within
This fire I kindle, now gently
Warming my heart, to begin

STAGES OF THE GRIEF PROCESS

It is important that we understand what is involved in the grief process. We will all go through it and many of us already have. As I see it, the stages include:

1. *Shock.* This is the body/mind's way of saving us from the devastating pain of the loss, at least initially. It is a blessing at best, but at worst can become a long-term numbness to feelings that resembles a sort of living death.

2. *Denial.* This is our mind's attempt to protect us from the reality of the loss. We may lie to ourselves and think about the person as if they were still alive. A certain period of denial is normal but if prolonged, it can keep us stuck and prevent resolution. There are many forms of denial, as varied as people are different from each other.

3. *Anger.* When we lose someone we love, it is natural to be angry for a period of time. We may be angry at the person for leaving us, angry at ourselves for what we did not do to save them (as in Ray's case) or angry at God for taking them away. We may just be angry at the unfairness and injustice of life.

4. *Guilt.* There seems to be a human tendency to blame ourselves when something happens to one we love. In loving someone, we automatically take some responsibility for their welfare. It is only natural to question ourselves for a period of time after our loved ones die. This is part of the normal grief process, but it is extremely important that we move through and don't get stuck in this stage. Again, Ray's situation offers an example of what happens when one gets stuck in the guilt stage of grieving.

5. *Pain And Sorrow.* These feelings often exist throughout the entire grief process. In the early stages, however, we are often distracted by denial, anger, guilt and the resulting confusion. To truly face and experience the pain and sorrow is healthy, and it moves us forward in the grief process. It is possible to become stuck in this stage but if so, there is usually some unresolved guilt and anger involved.

6. *Release And Resolution.* This stage of the grief process is accompanied by a sense of acceptance of the reality of the loss, a sense of "letting go." The denial, guilt and anger stages are over, and the pain and sorrow is not as intense as it was before. Many people ask, "How long does it take?" The answer is different according to the severity of the loss and the health of the individual who is grieving. Grieving moves in cy-

cles, and it may seem as if we are through for a substantial period of time. A birthday, anniversary or another loss can bring back many of the same feelings that were there when our loved one died. Any loss or low emotional period can bring back the feelings of loss, particularly if we have not reached resolution.

7. *Return To the Willingness To Love.* This is the final stage of the grieving process. Healing has occurred, and the grieving person is able to laugh again and to get involved in life. This occurs through an appreciation for ourselves and the life we are left to live. Nurturing our inner child is an excellent tool to use to help us through the grief process. Part of the return to love also includes remembering the love we felt for the one we lost. The love lives on and the anger, guilt, pain and sorrow fade away.

This stage of the grief process is ultimately a spiritual one. It is a fact that all of us on this planet will die. We need to have some way of living, laughing and loving with this reality. That's where spirituality comes in. True security cannot be found in another person. We have to turn within, to our own concept of the infinite, to ultimately find peace and security in a life that is only temporary in its tangible form.

I would also like to add another important comment about grief work. The approach I have briefly outlined here can be applied to many kinds of losses. Here is a list of losses many of us suffer which necessitate a period of grieving:

Death
Divorce
Loss of innocence through physical or sexual abuse
Loss of respect for our body because of abuse
Loss of love through abandonment or rejection
Loss of childhood through being required to take on
    too much responsibility too soon in life
Loss of health through illness, injury or aging
Loss of community through a geographical move.

You may be able to think of other types of losses which you or others may have suffered. The important point to keep in mind is that we are not victims of these losses for the rest of our lives. We can take charge by moving through our own individual form of grief to a point of peace and resolution, while growing and learning in the process.

GETTING UNSTUCK WITH ANGER

Ray was angry. The only problem was that he was angry at himself. His suicide attempts had been violent and extreme. He once said maybe the reason he had lived through them was that he wasn't ready to put himself out of his misery until he had suffered some more. Sometimes during sessions he would hit his leg so hard there would be a bruise that lasted two weeks.

Ray was very resistant to doing anger work. My thought was that he secretly knew it would help. His guilt would not allow him to get better. Finally he agreed, only because I gave him permission to direct the anger toward himself in the words he used.

We were in the Grief And Loss group at the hospital, and the other group members were very supportive of Ray releasing his anger. One of the most significant parts of this type of healing is the love and support of fellow patients who have cried, raged, laughed and loved together. I feel this was an important key to the process that got Ray on to the mat that Tuesday morning.

"Come on, Ray, you can do it! Get mad, you'll feel a lot better." This came from a man who had his first rage release experience in the preceding Anger Management group. All the members were leaning forward, cheering him on. Ray sat on his heels with fists clenched, staring at the mat in front of him.

"Hit the mat and say 'It's my fault!' " I coached from the sidelines. I knew he could only express anger toward himself at this point. My strategy was that he would eventually get past this belief and connect with the deeper anger he had toward his father for leaving him at home to care for his mother while he and Ray's brothers went to football games and had fun. When he finally started hitting the mat, I had to stop him several times from switching to hitting himself. After several sessions, however, he suddenly screamed in the middle of pounding the mat, "It was *not* my fault! I was too young to be doing that! It was your job, you good-for-nothing bastard!" (Language in anger work often gets quite colorful.)

I knew Ray was going to make it now. He had gone back to the beginning point of his guilt and was shaking its foundation. He still had a lot of work to do, but the self-hatred had ended. His anger had been a tool to break through what was the biggest wall of guilt I had ever witnessed. He was beginning to experience anger on his own behalf for the first time in his life. This was his first movement in the direction of self-love, which was essential for resolving his lifetime of guilt and arrested grief.

BEGINNING AND ENDING WITH LOVE

In Figure 7.1 you will see the concentric circle diagram as it applies to the grief process. You might envision the process as moving out from the center to the edge and back again.

It all starts with the experience of loving and being loved. When we lose, we feel pain and sorrow, the next ring in the circles. Although we didn't talk about fear as part of the grief process, it is easy to see where it fits in. Because we loved and lost, we fear loving and losing again.

The next ring contains guilt, anger and denial, which are all seen here as forms of protection or — more accurately in some cases — distraction from pain, fear and sorrow.

The outer ring involves the strength, skill, knowledge and awareness necessary to go back inside, through the walls of protection and distraction (picking up a little empowerment from our healthy anger), past the fear, through the pain and sorrow, returning finally to the

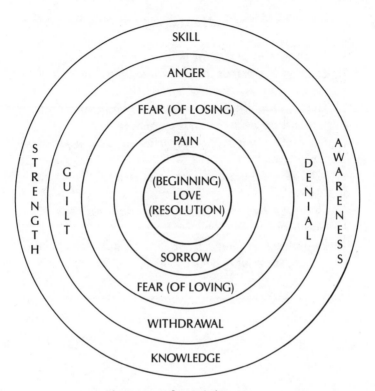

Figure 7.1. The Grief Process

center of love — for ourselves and for those we lost. From this perspective, we might say that the grief process begins and ends with love.

There is much more that could be said about grieving and the grief process. The focus here has been on the stages and the role of anger in helping to bring about resolution. I encourage you to educate yourself on the grief process and work toward resolution in your own life. The skills involved can be learned and mastered, so you do not have to live in fear of losing those you love.

To love means to risk the pain of losing.
Grieving is a process which I am willing to learn and experience as a natural part of my life.
The joy and fulfillment of loving and being loved are worth the pain and sorrow of losing.
The depth of my pain is proportionate to the depth of my love.
If I had not loved and been loved, I would know no sorrow.
Only love lives on as sorrow comes and goes.
Love is the deepest of all emotions.
Empowered by love, I move through all of my pain and fear, coming finally to a place of inner peace.

8

Male Anger —
From The Raging Bull
To The Wild Man

*(I will be talking directly to male readers for
much of this chapter, and I apologize to female readers
for the seeming discourtesy. I feel the issue of male anger is
a crucial one which needs to be addressed directly.
I trust both men and women will find value
in the discussion of it.)*

When we think of anger, the face of a furious, raging
man often comes to mind. The thought of an angry man
is not a pleasant one. Throughout history, we have been
taught to fear, avoid and even hate this image of male
anger. This is for good reason. Wars have been caused by
such men, corrupted by power and controlled by their
emotions, acting out their rage on millions of human beings they never met. How can we as men ever feel good

about our anger in the face of this image of a violent, raging maniac who has done so much harm? How can we face our own suppressed emotions when we fear that such a violent rage exists deep within us?

In our country we have moved the angry male from the war front to the home front. Without the distraction of a war until only recently, we have become painfully aware of how many men abuse and molest their children and wives. The shame and fear a man feels at the mere prospect of facing and embracing his anger as a valid emotion is tremendous and seemingly insurmountable. So the suppression continues.

Suppression, of course, leads to a couple of different alarming consequences. One is the inevitable explosion and loss of control that comes when the rage reaches a boiling point. In such cases, suppression leads to more abuse and violence. The other result of stuffing anger is illness and eventually premature death. It is my opinion that the reason men die younger than women is related to our tendency to suppress our emotions and — even worse — hate ourselves for having them. To get a feel for this, go visit a rest home sometime. You will find that the majority of the residents are female and widows.

So here we are, on the horns of a dilemma. To live longer, to claim our emotions, we must face our fear and shame associated with male anger. We must learn to transform the Raging Bull into the gentle but powerful Wild Man.

THE RAGING BULL

We had just met. He was big and muscular, with blood-shot eyes. I don't remember his name. He was in my Anger Management group at the hospital, and he was paying very close attention. When he spoke, he was vague about his own situation. He implied, however, that he was afraid of hurting his wife and child. I never found out whether he already had. He watched closely as some other patients did anger work. When I asked if he wanted to try it, he said, "Not now. Could I talk with you for a few minutes after the group?" I agreed, not knowing what to expect. When I left the group room, he was standing there waiting for me. Without even thinking about it, I asked if he wanted to do some anger work with me in private. He nodded immediately, as if he had been impatiently waiting for this moment for a long time.

When we got into the seclusion room, where individual anger work is done at the hospital, I started my usual demonstration and explanation. I did not get a chance to finish. I barely got out of the way in time, before he started the most amazing rage release I have ever witnessed.

This man, who weighed well over 200 pounds, left the floor entirely. He had been kneeling at the end of the mat, staring at it and ignoring me. His fists went into the air and his body stretched out full length, as he actually left the floor before crashing with amazing force onto the mat. With almost no hesitation, he did it again. Somehow he had the energy to propel his entire body into the air, before hitting the mat with all of his force and fury.

He roared. That's the only word that fits. The sound that came from him emanated from deep in his chest. Spit flew from his mouth as a lifetime of rage exploded from this huge, powerful man. After three or four of these "body slams," he went back to a kneeling position at the end of the mat. Now he was growling. A low rumble rolled up from the same deep place inside him that had released the roar.

"I've got to get rid of the bull. It's killing me, and if I let it out, it will kill someone else," he rasped between deep breaths, with no prompting from me. I asked, "Where did you get it?"

"From my father," he whispered between growls. "Give it back to him," I said with intense feeling. His energy had a profound effect on me. I felt connected to him in his process.

The words were barely out of my mouth before he was back in the air again. This time he went even longer — crashing, pounding, roaring, screaming, "Get out of me!

Take it back, you sorry son-of-a-bitch! I'm through! I never asked for it, and it's not me!"

I was impressed with his words. They were the same words I would have suggested for him to use if he had asked for my guidance. I knew something powerful and important was happening, and I was just a witness. My primary role was to support him and, most importantly, not to be afraid of him.

When we finally went back out into the hall, the staff and patients seemed in a state of shock. They, like me, had never heard anything like the sounds this man produced in that room. He looked at me and said, "Thanks, Doc. The bull is gone."

I only saw him one more time before he left the hospital. He was on the phone as I walked by. He looked up, smiled and made the "Everything is A-OK" hand sign. I haven't heard any more from him or about him, but I intuitively feel that he is just fine. I think I saw the raging bull leave him that day after group and somehow we both knew it would never be back.

His raging bull was released and no one was hurt. This was the first time. Every other time the bull had come out, it had frightened, hurt, wounded and abused whoever was close by. That was primarily his family. The shame and guilt were healed because the release had caused no injury. He had discovered the innocence and harmlessness of the emotion that charged and powered the bull.

NO GURLS ALOWD

Remember those books when we were kids about the boys building secret clubhouses where the girls couldn't come? There was a period of our late childhood and early adolescence when (God forbid!) girls were actually bigger than us. Word had it that they got smarter earlier than we did, too. No wonder we had to develop some camaraderie among ourselves just to maintain a little dignity as guys! Cub and Boy Scouts provided some of these opportunities, but many of us just worked it out in the neighborhood. We weren't ready or able to date yet, and forming same-sex social groups was natural and easy.

There is a popular theory of developmental psychology, presented by H.S. Sullivan in *The Interpersonal Theory Of Psychiatry*, which says that boys and girls both go through a stage during pre-adolescence when they prefer the company of the same sex. Some kissing and sexual play often occur during this phase of development as a natural and even healthy way of safely experimenting in the mysterious world of physical intimacy. If you remember such experiences, you may have some fear and guilt associated with them. It is very common for men in particular to have strong fears of being homosexual because of childhood experimentation. If you have such fears, take this opportunity to relieve your anxiety. It is okay. It was just a stage which most of us go through as a part of growing up.

DEVELOPMENT OF THE AMERICAN MALE

If our fathers were absent, drunk or otherwise emotionally unavailable, we had little support in working through this somewhat confusing aspect of development. It was Dad's job to provide a role model for us, showing what it means to be a man, to be masculine. Of course, he most likely did not receive this from his own father, which is why he wasn't there for us.

In the absence of Dad's guidance, we had to wing it, which means we got it from TV, movies and comic books. We learned about being men from John Wayne, Spider Man, Superman, Sergeant Rock of Easy Company, Matt Dillon and for younger readers, Dirty Harry and Rambo. Even if we did have a father figure around, he most likely had role models with the same kind of limitations.

So, coming out of this developmental stage, we had to get tough (like our heroes) and we had to show this to each other and to the girls. Thus came the birth of macho in the American male. Remember how cruel we were to each other as adolescents (and this applies to both male

and female), particularly in junior high school? This is
one of the ways we worked our way out of the awkward
stage of development when we didn't like the opposite
sex. What a price we paid! Some of my worst memories
are from those years when social acceptance seemed a
matter of life and death.

Behind the false front of the macho man is a scared,
confused little boy who was never supported and guided
through his own emotional, sexual and social adjustment.
You are probably aware that the macho male social scene
includes jokes and slurs about women and homosexuals.
This seems to follow naturally from the unresolved sexual
development of early adolescence and the absence of appropriate male role models.

The situation becomes pretty serious when you consider
the consequences of adolescent men playing with millions
of dollars, world politics and nuclear weapons. It is also
sobering to look at the kinds of fathers and husbands so
many of us turned out to be. Being stuck with a seriously-
lacking macho male image to fulfill, we find ourselves
severely handicapped when it comes to expressing the true
intimate feelings necessary for healthy relationships.

THE ONLY TWO EMOTIONS ALLOWED

As males, we got the basic message that it is okay to be
angry. But we also learned that it is not, I repeat *not okay*
to show fear or pain or sorrow. We were shown plenty of
male anger on TV and in the movies. It was almost always
violent and aggressive — even deadly. As a matter of
fact, male anger was often what saved the day for the
good guys. The only time we saw fear or pain was in the
faces and voices of the bad guys, just as the hero was
about to "get" them. The implication is, of course, that if
we show or even feel fear or pain, we are weak and will
be destroyed.

Most of us rarely, if ever, saw our fathers cry. If we did,
it was by accident and he was most likely ashamed of
himself for "losing control" or "breaking down." The pow-

erful suggestion is that we are never to be vulnerable or acknowledge our deeper, more private feelings. This means basically that we can't be emotionally close to another person, male or female. If you look at Figure 8.1, you will get a picture of what happens when intimacy stops at the level of defense and protection. Sure, we get to hide (and deny) our fear and pain, but look at what is in the center. In hiding our fear and pain, we severely limit our ability to love. Another way of saying this is that, if we can't face our own fear, we are not strong enough to risk the vulnerability of opening our hearts in true intimate love.

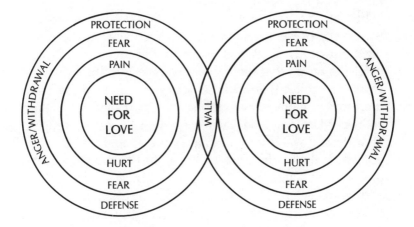

Figure 8.1. The Wall Of Defensiveness

The other emotion we were allowed as males was a limited kind of love. It had to be love for a female, and it had to be sexual. Thus the sexist aspects of the macho male. With only anger and sexually-oriented love as acceptable emotions, we became emotional cripples as men, with a tremendous amount of unmet needs. Getting aggressive or having sex have been our only two options for emotional release and relief of tension. When we combine these two emotions, sexual love and anger, we have major problems.

I believe this explains much of the physical and sexual abuse perpetrated by men on children, as well as women. It cannot be overemphasized how important it is that we deal with this as men. It is something we have to work out together — we can't get it from women. We have leaned on women to meet our emotional needs for a long time now, and it isn't fair to women.

Just as our fathers were absent, most of our mothers were very present, and we were dependent on them to meet our needs. They had to try (and of necessity, fail) to meet the needs that our fathers were neglecting by their absence. I think this made us angry at our mothers and therefore at women, even though it wasn't their fault. We blamed Mom for Dad's absence, in many cases, simply because she was there and an easy scapegoat. Dad was out saving the world, bringing home the bacon or however that was explained in our own home. However, they were both responsible for what occurred in our home.

Now the picture is complete. We have groups of grown-up adolescent men playing with expensive toys and making derogatory jokes about women and sex. Consequences range from world war and wife-beating to boring social lives and lousy marriages. Consequences also include depression, anxiety and early death due to stress-related illnesses. It is time we did something about this, men. If we don't, no one will.

If you are not already aware, you need to know there is a new men's movement going on in this country. We are starting to break free from the stifling, ugly, limiting and even deadly image of the American male.

AWAKENING THE WILD MAN

In talking about our potential for growth together as men, I defer to the authority, wisdom and experience of Robert Bly.

As a poet, storyteller and facilitator of men's workshops throughout the United States, Robert Bly is breaking new ground. With the help of a growing number of associates, he is paving the way for the creation of a completely new set of ideas about what it means to be male. I, for one, am very grateful for the work he has done.

One of the stories Bly tells is the myth of *Iron John*, which is also the title of his latest book. The message is that deep within the male psyche is an ancient hairy man. Contacting this Wild Man is risky and scary. He is under the water of man's soul, and no one has visited there for a long time. Our experiences with anger and violence cause us to fear that the Wild Man will be violent and aggressive. But he is neither.

As described by Bly, the Wild Man is forceful and acts with resolve. He is not cruel, nor opposed to others. He is also not controlled by others and their expectations. The Wild Man is unpredictable. He is guided by an inner spirit which is uniquely his own as manifested in his thoughts, words and actions. The deep dark aspects of the Wild Man's home represent the sensitive receptive aspects of the male, so long rejected as not being masculine.

Releasing the Wild Man within means facing all of the emotions surrounding love — including love of life, music, poetry, art and nature. The word "wild" in this context implies untamed, uncontained and uncontrolled by external forces. Picture the business executive with the pin-striped navy blue suit, white shirt, red tie and serious facial expression. Where's the Wild Man? However deeply he may be buried, he is never completely absent. Each of us can awaken the spontaneous, creative spirit within, whatever our background may have been. To make the mysterious journey within, we must be willing to face and deal with all of our emotions.

Let's say you are with me so far, and we are seeing eye to eye on most of this. It seems we are caught between fear of being the embarrassingly adolescent macho male and the seemingly worse alternative — the dreaded wimp. If our fathers were passive, or if our mothers were, and they served as our role models, we may have some passive tendencies ourselves. Sometimes being passive is a reaction to an abusive or violent father. The decision: "I'll never be like him, no matter what!" often breeds passivity in the son of an angry father. As we saw in the story of Paul in Chapter Three, passivity becomes a prison which stifles, suppresses and sometimes leads to violent outbursts.

Fortunately, we don't have to choose between macho and wimp. We are very new at this, but the image of a new healthy man is beginning to emerge.

A HEALTHY ADULT MAN

He laughs easily. His smile is relaxed as if it belongs there on his face. He is at home in his body. He may not be in perfect shape but he is not extremely out of shape, either. When alone or lost in his own thoughts, he looks interested and thoughtful, not worried or afraid. He takes care of himself.

He works hard when he works, but he knows how to stop. He is successful at what he does, and he enjoys doing it. He wouldn't do it if he didn't enjoy it. He is motivated by a sense of purpose, by his own values and ideals. He is not governed by the demands and expectations of society or even those close to him. He is sensitive to what is required to be a part of a functioning society, and he does not break the law. He is also sensitive to the emotional needs of loved ones and responds skillfully and effectively. He does what he feels is right for himself and others concerned, based on the situation at hand. He is capable of feeling desire and following this feeling. He trusts his own intuition and judgment, and also takes full responsibility for his mistakes. He is guided by a profound sense of spiritual purpose which emanates from deep within his being.

He is considered reliable by his friends and associates. They know he would not agree to something if he did not intend to follow through. He knows how to say no. He is consistent and flexible at the same time. Some aspects of his life are structured and disciplined, while there are times when he seems to be a totally new and different person. He is capable of surprising even those who know him best. He is always growing and changing. He is not afraid of change and the challenges brought about in transition. He can lead and he can follow. He does not seem to care which he does, but he does want to move. If the available leadership is ineffective, he will not follow. If no one follows his own leadership, he will re-evaluate his direction and focus. If he finds that he is still committed, he will continue alone.

He is fully and completely an adult man. He has dealt with his unresolved childhood issues and knows how to meet his own emotional needs. He feels no guilt or shame. He can talk openly, when appropriate, about his own pain, fear and need for love. He expresses his love openly for those who are important to him. He can talk comfortably and easily about his pain and his fear. He also expresses his anger.

When angry, he becomes clear and precise in his communication. He may raise his voice, but only slightly, so the listener will get the message. The person on the receiving end knows that he means what he says. If his anger builds and he feels tense and irritable, he withdraws to a safe place and works out the physical tension in a way that suits him. This may be with anger work such as is described in this book, or it may be relaxing, meditating, writing, reading, sleeping or exercising. When he is physically calm and clear as to what he intends to say, he goes back and expresses his feelings verbally to the appropriate people. He never blames anyone for his feelings or his problems. He takes full responsibility for himself as a person and for his needs and feelings.

He is creative. Being creative is a spiritual process for him. He believes creativity is something that flows through him, using the resources he has available for expression.

He is spiritually focused, though he does not talk very often in spiritual terms. He may be a part of an organized religion, though if he is, he does not restrict his beliefs to the confines of the organization and its doctrine. His spiritual faith is a private matter to him, although he does share his views with a select group of people. He has nothing to prove, and he has no need to convince anyone of anything. He respects the right of everyone to believe as they choose and expects the same respect for himself. His spiritual life is the center of his existence. He is aware of eternity. His deity is a loving, all-knowing, all-powerful God.

He knows how to play and be childlike when the time or mood is right. A sense of joy periodically and regularly rises from within him. He is comfortable with children and with animals, and they enjoy him as well. He can feel at home in a penthouse at the top of a New York skyscraper or alone on top of a mountain. The world is his home. He is glad to be here.

As a man, I am a vast mystery.

I am in the process of discovering what it means to be a joyous, healthy man.

I accept all of my emotions, especially my pain and my fear.

By claiming my pain and my fear, I am taking charge of them.

When I am in charge of my feelings, I am in charge of my life.

As a man, it is important that I be open and receptive.

I am sensitive and responsive in relationships with men and women.

I am in charge of my life.

I am open to the deep and magical aspects of who I am.

I am at peace and at home in the world.

9

Releasing Anger In Healthy Ways

Healthy expression of anger is a rare occurrence. Most of us don't know what anger is when it is expressed in healthy ways. Pure and simple, anger is energy — emotional energy. It can turn into determination and motivation to get something done in spite of seemingly insurmountable odds. When managed and directed in a constructive manner, anger is our ally in time of need. Your anger can be your friend.

Anger is expressed both verbally and non-verbally.

ANGER LIVES IN YOUR BODY, NOT IN YOUR BRAIN

There are some simple exercises you can use to release the physical tension associated with your anger. By doing this, you will become more relaxed and better able to think and communicate verbally. The build-up of physical and emotional tension actually blocks our minds from clear thinking and prevents effective communication. Therefore, the first thing we must do when we are extremely angry is to release the physical energy or "blow off some steam." This is done primarily through the use of the techniques I will describe below.

These methods of anger release can produce some surprising results. It is important that anyone using them to help another person be experienced and qualified in counseling and psychotherapy. As anger is released, pain, fear and often rage rise to the surface. It is important that all these emotions be processed effectively and with as much resolution as possible. The examples given throughout this book may have given you some idea of what happens when individuals with unresolved trauma from childhood use some of these methods.

It is not really necessary to warn you to avoid doing anger work if you're not ready. You just won't do it. My experience has been that each individual knows when there is a powder keg beneath the surface getting ready to blow. No one wants to voluntarily set off that explosion. That only happens when we "lose control." In other words, if you have unresolved rage, pain and fear, you will not be at all interested in doing anger work on your own or without the help of a trained professional.

We have all heard the phrase "talk it out" as a recommended way of resolving anger and other difficulties in relationships. This does work, but only if the physical and emotional components of the anger are in a state of balance and there is an internal sense of equilibrium. When we get angry, our bodies get hot, our muscles are tense, our hearts pound and our thoughts race out of control. This is not a time for trying to verbally communicate our feelings. This is a time to attend to our own internal physical and emotional needs until we can relax enough to think clearly. Only then can we begin to communicate effectively with another person about what is going on. Our emotions live in our bodies, and our minds are merely

interpreters or messengers describing the feelings that
are pulsing within us from our heads to our toes.

HOW TO KNOW IF YOU HAVE
A PROBLEM WITH ANGER

Many of you already know that you have a problem
with anger. You may have known before reading this book
or you may have realized it while reading the preceding
chapters. For those of you who are not sure, here are
some indicators:

- When you get angry, you don't get over it. Sometimes
  it lasts until you explode or it may go inside to fuel
  the fires of your rage. You may be one who "holds a
  grudge."
- You never get angry. You just don't have the emotion.
  There are times when you know you *should* be angry,
  but the emotion just doesn't seem to come. Your anger
  is "watered down" and you never fully release it.
- You feel frustrated, disappointed or irritable much of
  the time, but you just don't ever get angry. Anger may
  be an unacceptable emotion, whereas frustration, disappointment or irritability are more acceptable,
  though not pleasant. This can interfere with or prevent any meaningful level of fulfillment or joy in life.
- You are sarcastic or cynical about yourself, others or
  the world around you. You may tease others with
  "velvet daggers" in some of your "jokes," only to be
  surprised when they don't want to be around you.
  You don't openly express anger but it is leaking out all
  the time.
- You may be depressed frequently and for long periods
  of time. You don't express anger openly but take it out
  on yourself, whether you realize it or not. This can
  lead to suicidal thoughts and behavior or perhaps major illness. Paul Pearsall, in his book *Superimmunity*,
  makes the point that our immune system is less func-

tional during periods of emotional depression, thereby making us more susceptible to disease.

- Perhaps you are angry all the time. You may be verbally, emotionally or even physically abusive to others in personal and professional relationships. This doesn't mean that you are a bad person, but it is certainly time that you learned to manage your anger. You could begin to deal with your anger and express it in ways that do not hurt anyone. If you have indeed been abusive, it is almost certain that you will need professional help to work through your problems with anger.
- You feel powerless in your own life — powerless to make the changes you choose to reach your goals. Though you may not use the word, you feel like a victim much of the time. You probably have many ways to explain why you can't live your dreams, all of which seem very reasonable to you. The point is that if you are denying your power by denying your emotions, you are getting in your own way. To claim all of your emotions as your allies, and to express them completely in healthy ways, is to maximize your resources for your own expression of purpose in your life.

If you have decided that any of these examples apply to you, then it's a safe bet that you have suppressed anger or even rage. For this reason it is important that you know what to expect if you choose to do anger work, either on your own or with help.

SPACE, EQUIPMENT AND SUPPLIES NEEDED:

Fortunately not much is needed in the way of equipment. A mattress or large overstuffed pillow will usually suffice. If you're using an exercise mat, you definitely need a pillow, as most mats are just not soft enough. It is *very* important that precautions be taken to avoid injury. After all, the point is to provide an experience of expressing anger in a way that doesn't hurt anyone, including the person doing the anger work.

These exercises need to be done in private, unless you are with a trained professional or in a therapy group with a professional present. Your family and friends usually won't understand, and you don't need to be questioned about what you are doing. As much as possible you need to feel safe. I usually advise clients who choose to do this at home to do so when they are alone in their house — unless their spouse understands and supports the anger work.

Some people do anger work alone in their car. Although this is better than taking it out on another person, it can be dangerous and I don't advise it. If you feel you are going to explode, however, it may be more healthy to scream alone in your car than to suppress your anger and hurt yourself — or stuff it until you explode at someone you love.

Another piece of equipment sometimes useful in anger release work is a *bataca* or "encounter bat." These are foam-padded bats which can be ordered through special supply houses which handle therapeutic equipment. The bat is sometimes helpful to people with back problems who might have a problem hitting a mat or pillow with their fists or arms. It also allows an opportunity for the person to feel more powerful and in control.

If a "body bag" or sand-filled canvas punching bag is used, it is important to use some type of gloves to avoid scraping the skin off your knuckles. Using gloves may also be necessary if hitting a vinyl mat with your clenched fists. The upright bag, either suspended from the ceiling or leaned into a corner, is sometimes helpful for those who would rather stand than kneel in the anger release process. If the bag is suspended from the ceiling, it needs to be somehow anchored to the floor. This is to prevent the delay in your release work as you wait for the bag to swing back in your direction. To achieve a complete release, we need to be able to have a full-blown explosion, and this can't be accomplished if we have to wait and plan our blows to a swinging punching bag.

THE UPRIGHT POSITION

In the early stages of anger work many people are stuck in blaming someone else for their anger. This is natural, of course, particularly when we have been hurt or abused by someone else's behavior. When this is the case, people usually want to do their anger work standing up and want to picture the face of the person they are blaming on the mat or bag. I do not encourage this but it is better to allow a person to try this method of release than to cause them to continue to suppress their anger.

Matt checked into the hospital to keep from killing his boss. He was certain that if he had stayed out and continued to go to work, he would have committed murder. When he came to my Anger Management group, he insisted that his anger existed only because of what his boss had done. He refused to claim responsibility for his emotions and refused to try any of the anger-release methods I recommended. As his discharge date approached, I gave in to his request for a private session in which he planned to hit a mat up against the wall while picturing his boss's face and body on the mat. He did this with lots of profanity and seething hatred. He did not experience any type of emotional release, and he told me the next day that he didn't feel any better. As a matter of fact, he said he hated his boss more than ever.

This is an example of the results of blaming. When we blame others for our anger, fear and pain, we are giving them all of our power. This is a difficult lesson. It seems we each need to learn it over and over throughout our lives. Matt was beginning to learn this lesson for the first time.

He was so afraid of leaving the hospital with his feelings of rage and hatred unresolved that he finally agreed to try some anger-release work in the ways I recommended. In the seclusion room the last day before his discharge, I got him to talk about his feelings toward his father as he was growing up. Immediately the same feelings of rage and hatred began to surface. This time, however, I got him to acknowledge that the feelings were his responsibility alone, that they had been with him all of his life. Before I conclude Matt's story, I want to make a few more comments about the upright methods of anger release. I still recommend this position for those with back problems or for those to whom the other positions are too threatening at first. My primary concern about this position is that it requires people to use their fists. This does not allow the powerful release that is accomplished in the two methods I will describe below. There is also serious risk of injury to the wrists, knuckles and fingers with a straight-on punching technique. If this position is used, cautious advice should be given and the person should be encouraged to move to one of the safer positions as soon as possible.

THE POWER POSITION

I refer to this technique as the "power position" only because I have seen so many people claim their power over their lives and emotions while using this method. It seems to be the position that most people are the least uncomfortable with when first trying anger-release work.

The power position first involves kneeling on the end of a bed, mattress or soft mat. The person's knees should be on the mat, not on the floor. Many people are not accustomed to resting their weight on the knees, and a cushion helps to relieve some of the pressure on the joints. The ideal arrangement is to have a large, well-stuffed pillow directly in front of the knees. This position is difficult or impossible for those with back trouble, and it is necessary to be aware of these types of problems before trying this technique.

After the person is kneeling on the mat, I usually tell them to raise their arms directly over their head, make fists with both hands, and come down on the pillow or mat as hard as they can. I recommend that the actual blow be struck with the entire lower arm, from the elbow to the fist. This allows for a more powerful energy release than using fists.

I only have an opportunity to give this coaching, by the way, in a few cases. Most of the time once a person has hit a few times, the anger and rage surfaces and they are not hearing or seeing anything. If a person is using their fists, I don't stop them to correct the procedure. I try to exert as little control in their process as possible. The point is to offer support and safety for them while they "lose control" for the first time without hurting themselves or someone else. If there is a pause while they are catching their breath, I will advise them to try using their entire lower arm if they have been using their fists. Again, hitting with fists presents the risk of injury to knuckles and wrists.

Occasionally I have found some individuals more comfortable sitting on the mat with their legs extended in front of them. In this position there is less stress on the knees, but for some it may create more back strain. The hitting in this position is actually done on the mat between the extended legs. I have also known some people to use open hands in this position, which is an option to using closed fists. I usually recommend using closed fists, because it is a more powerful hand position and because hitting with open hands is sometimes painful, particularly on a vinyl mat.

I have had a couple of experiences with facilitating anger work for individuals with severe back, hip and leg problems. For these individuals, sitting in their chair or wheelchair while hitting another chair with an encounter bat seems to work fairly well. I have also found that some people are more physically comfortable holding a pillow in their own lap and hitting it with both fists or open hands.

Matt finally agreed to use the power position. Kneeling on the mat, he began breathing heavily. It was as if his body knew it was about to explode and release a lifetime of rage. He exploded all right. By the time he was through, he was sweating and breathing so heavily it took him half an hour to recover enough to stand up and walk out of the room. But now he was smiling. He didn't explain his smile, and I'm not sure he could have if he had tried. The smile wasn't coming from his brain; it was coming from his body. His heart was relieved of more than 40 years of pressure, tension and pain. The next day he gave me an update. "Well, I'm still angry, but I don't want to kill anybody. I know what I'm going to do about the situation at work, and I'm doing it for me and my family, not for revenge on my boss. I feel more in touch with myself than I have since I hit my first home run at fourteen." Matt shook my hand and thanked me, but he did not give anyone but himself credit for what he had accomplished — and rightfully so. I have long ago learned I can't force anyone to work who does not want to. He did his part, so he was able to reach his goal.

THE TEMPER TANTRUM TECHNIQUE

This posture for anger release allows a full body rage release that seems to go deeper into the body and thus deeper into the subconscious mind. When a person is having difficulty with the power position or if they have used the power position several times and still have not reached the "bottom" of their rage, I strongly recommend this technique. It is based on the position and method many of us have seen demonstrated by very young children. Some of us may even remember doing it ourselves.

This method of rage and anger release involves lying on one's back on a mattress or mat that is wide enough to allow at least eight to twelve inches clearance on both sides of the body. This is to provide space for pounding with both hands without going off the mat. While releasing anger in this way, the person's body will sometimes drift off to one side or the other or up or down on the mat. If the mat does not allow enough room for this, the person will go off the edge or ends of the mat, which will interrupt the flow of their emotional release.

The procedure begins with the person closing their eyes. I then instruct them to raise their feet up on the mat so their legs are bent and their feet are flat on the surface of the mat. The next step is to begin pounding alternately with both hands and kicking alternately with both feet. For most people this involves hitting with the right fist while kicking with the right foot, then hitting with the left fist while kicking with the left foot. For a full release, the person must do this as rapidly as possible until their body takes over and they don't have to think about what they are doing at all. Usually not much instruction is needed, since the subconscious mind remembers everything, including how to throw a good temper tantrum.

VOCAL AND VERBAL COMPONENTS OF ANGER WORK

Voice tone and volume, as well as words and phrases spoken, are extremely important components of anger-release work. Regarding volume, the rule is the louder the better. The reason for this is that greater volume tends to open up the entire vocal capacity, allowing the voice to come from the diaphragm and chest region rather than from the throat. There is also less likelihood of damaging the throat or vocal chords when the throat muscles are relaxed and the voice is being projected from deep within the midsection.

Our voice has always been a primary means of expressing emotions. In other words, our voice is a primary means of expressing ourselves. It is suppression of emotion, suppression of self, that leads to the need for anger-release work. Many of us were told to "shut up" as children, and we need to overcome this message to our subconscious mind. As our anger and other emotions are suppressed, there is an inevitable suppression of our sense of self-worth. Thus in doing anger work we are not only beginning to reclaim our emotions, we are beginning to reclaim ourselves.

In the power position, the basic statement I recommend for starters is *"I'm angry!"* This needs to be said with as much feeling as possible. There are infinite variations in the appropriate words and phrases to use with different individuals, and the decision-making process I go through to choose the best words for effective release is based on my entire career of practicing psychotherapy. For this reason, I am not going to try to give you a list of the best verbalizations to use in your own or your clients' anger work. It is simply too complex to go into in this introductory volume. I emphasize this point so readers will not believe that after learning about these techniques, they will be prepared to provide intensive anger and rage release interventions.

I again emphasize that these methods should only be used by trained and qualified professionals, licensed to practice psychotherapy in their state of residence. If you want to try the techniques yourself, you can obviously accept full responsibility for the results. Experimenting with these powerful techniques on another person's emotions is another matter altogether.

VERBALIZATIONS

Appropriate verbalizations during anger work fall into three general categories. They are as follows:

1. Simple anger release phrases for the purpose of claiming the emotion, such as, "I'm *angry!*" (It is very common at this point to move into hatred toward the abusers or the people who abandoned or neglected them. If the person insists on saying, "I hate you," I will allow this. I move them on to more empowering statements as quickly as possible, however, because hatred is an insidious form of anger which is more harmful to the person feeling it than to the person being hated.)

2. Statements of fact which the person needs to acknowledge, as in the case of an incest or physical abuse victim saying, "It was *wrong!*" or "It wasn't my *fault!*"

3. In the case of a person who is having recurrent memories or flashbacks of an incident of abuse, it is sometimes helpful to have them visualize the incident while hitting the mat and say, *"Stop* it!" "Get *away!"* or "No *more!"* while picturing the abuser ceasing the abusive behavior. This is a powerful technique, as it couples the physical and emotional power of the victim's anger with an assertion against the acts of the abuser. This is often a corrective process which eliminates flashbacks and recurrent nightmares. By claiming strength in this way, the person is for the first time moving out of the victim position in relation to the abuser.

4. If there is fear, shame, self-blame or another type of interference to the effective release of anger, a statement of the fear or mental block can sometimes help to remove it. Examples of such block-removal statements would be, "I'm *afraid!"* "I can't *feel!"* or "It's *my* fault!" To go even deeper into the shame and to release it, the statements, "I'm bad," "I am worthless" or "I'm a mistake" can be used. After these statements are repeated over and over, the block is usually removed, the truth begins to emerge and the fear or self-blame dissipates. The negative or block-removal statements are replaced with the appropriate alternative, such as, "I'm *strong!"* "I *can* feel!" or "It *wasn't* my *fault!"*

5. Other statements which are messages to caregivers in cases of neglect and abandonment are, "Where *were* you?" "I *needed* you!" or "Please *love* me!" These statements are particularly helpful in getting individuals in touch with their pain in order to facilitate the healing process that must always follow effective anger work.

6. The final category of statements to use in anger work that is specifically for the purpose of empowerment falls under the general heading of affirmations. In such cases it has been determined therapeutically that the person is ready to claim power

and affirm it emotionally and physically. Statements would be made such as, "It's *my* life!" "I *deserve* to be angry!" "I *deserve* to be loved!" "I am *lovable!*" "I'm a *good* person!" "I was a *good* child!" "I am *innocent!*" or "My body is *good!*"

If the person is not ready to fully accept the truth of these affirmations, they will not fully exert all of their physical and emotional energy while making the statements and hitting the mat. At that point they may be aware of a new block or interfering thought, which needs to be stated forcefully and worked through. Whenever the opportunity presents itself, anger work ideally ends with loud forceful statements of self-affirmation, in order that the body and mind is directing its energy in a positive direction. This may be done at the end of a session with someone who has made a major breakthrough, or at the end of a long period of treatment with someone who has been working through long-term healing in the process of dealing with major childhood trauma.

When using any of these verbalizations in anger work, one statement should be chosen at a time. This statement is repeated with each blow to the mat, with primary emphasis being placed on the word that is in italics in the examples given above. This seems to work best when the emphasized word is spoken forcefully at the instant the mat is hit. I usually have the individual repeat this process with as much power and momentum as possible, over and over until they are physically exhausted and need to rest.

The verbal statements described above are ordinarily used while the person is in the power position, and not in the more primal temper tantrum posture. In the latter position, I usually encourage individuals to open their mouths as wide as possible and scream or roar as loudly as they can. The instructions to roar usually prompt the person to move their voice down out of their throat and into their chest and diaphragm. As mentioned above, this is for the purpose of a more complete and primal release, as well as to avoid injury to the throat or vocal chords. When someone is on their back, hitting the mat with both hands and kicking with both feet while roaring from deep within their chest, you can rest assured that an effective release is occurring. People often report a life-long tension or pain in their stomach or chest is gone or reduced after this exercise. Better than any other method I know, this one seems to effectively get to the "bottom" of suppressed anger and rage.

EMOTIONAL REACTIONS TO EXPECT AND BE READY FOR

The reason I recommend caution in using these techniques is that I have seen almost every possible reaction occur according to individual physical, mental and emotional differences and variations in recovery process and personal history. At the end of the continuum where we find extreme trauma, you can expect any or all of the following:

1. *Nausea and possibly vomiting* after deep rage release. This reaction is the body's way of symbolically representing the process of purging and release that is occurring on an emotional level.

2. *Dissociation from current reality* and possibly from current identity. In most cases this can be effectively managed with sophisticated therapeutic techniques. However, in the case of individuals with dissociative or multiple personality disorders, the dissociation may need to continue temporarily until reintegration is possible and appropriate in terms of the patient's needs. Extreme caution and qualified supervision should always be employed when working with individuals with dissociative and multiple personality disorders.

3. *Self-destructive thought and behavior.* Often victims of extreme physical or sexual abuse will become suicidal

during or following rage work. The guilt they feel after becoming so enraged at their caregiver (even though that person was an abuser) throws them into shame, guilt and even self-hatred. John Bradshaw, in *Healing The Shame That Binds You*, makes the point that the abuse victim often will identify with the abuser to avoid the unmanageable conflict of hating a caregiver. Such people may sometimes try to injure themselves physically, thereby taking on the actual role of the abuser. It is the therapist's responsibility to ensure the person's safety from self-harm. When this type of response occurs, I immediately stop the rage and anger work and move into inner-child healing work or paradoxical therapeutic intervention to provide re-orientation and nurturing to the client.

4. *Paralysis in fear.* Some people can only go into their emotions as far as the fear and cannot penetrate far enough to reach their pain. Once again referring to the concentric circles of emotion in Figure 5.1, you can see that the empowerment of the anger only took the person as far as their wall of fear where they became paralyzed. When this occurs, it is essential that the individual be encouraged to do more anger work to empower themselves past the fear. This may happen in minutes, days or weeks after the first fear reaction, but it is the therapist's responsibility to see that the person does not stay stuck in fear. With persistence on the part of the therapist and encouragement to the patient, anger work for empowerment can always break through the fear, contact the pain and connect with the loving and lovable core of the individual.

As we move along the continuum toward less extreme trauma, we find more positive and easily attainable results such as:

1. **Emotional breakthrough.** This, fortunately, is one of the most common responses to anger release work. People feel the power of their own emotional and

physical strength, and they break through the fear. The pain is contacted, but as is shown in the concentric circle diagram in Figure 5.1, pain is directly connected to the need to give and receive love. The experience of feeling the pain is often experienced as compassion for the inner child as the person recognizes the injustice of what happened to them.

Some people stop in the pain and hold on to the anger, with new awareness of how they were abused, neglected or abandoned. This is encouraged as long as it is needed for empowerment. Eventually, the anger needs to be released in order for the person to be free from the victim position on an emotional and psychological level. Some individuals move more easily into a self-nurturing posture, which will be described in further detail below.

2. **Release, relief and return to joy.** Occasionally, though not often, an individual will break all the way through to the emotional center and contact joy, at the heart of their need to love and be loved. This is accompanied by experiences of empowerment, feelings of elation and a general sense of well-being. This rarely happens in the first anger release exercise, but if someone is consistent in their therapeutic work, it usually occurs at some point in the healing process. This is the goal of emotional release and regressive work.

A risk worth noting, however, is the tendency for therapist and patient alike to assume that this means therapy is over or that little is left to be done. Although this is indeed sometimes the case, it is far more common that contact with well-being and joy is simply a breakthrough from one stage to another, and there is still more work to be done.

As a matter of fact, these periods of well-being are sometimes followed by depression when the person is not cognitively ready to maintain an ongoing state of happiness. Guilt and shame sometimes flood in like a tidal wave if the person never had permission to feel these feelings of joy and self-love or if the family script was never to do better than the other family members. Once a person has had a taste of this, however, they know it is possible, and it provides motivation for further investment in growth and recovery.

VERBAL AND VISUAL MEMORIES AND HEALING WORK

While doing emotional release work, it is very common that a person will have sudden memories of events and conversations which were connected with the intense emotions being experienced. This is very helpful to the therapist as it provides material for healing and emotional/visual reconstruction.

The most accurate term to describe the methods I use after intense anger work is *inner-child healing work*. I do not have to induce any type of regression or trance state as the person is already in an altered state of consciousness due to the emotional release. I usually move directly into a visualization process in which the person pictures a traumatic childhood memory. This memory sometimes occurs spontaneously as mentioned above. Sometimes I facilitate the process by saying, "Can you see yourself as a child at a time when you were hurt or afraid and needed love?" When the patient has indicated that the memory is there, I have them fill in details until the picture is complete. Then I have them enter the situation as a powerful, loving adult. The task then is to move the abuser completely out of the picture in a firm and yet non-aggressive way. I encourage patients to do this by simply placing a hand on the chest of their abusers and pushing them out of the picture until they are completely gone or out of view.

Next I ask patients to carry their new-found love and strength to the frightened, wounded inner child. I encourage them to pick up the child and offer nurturance, love and protection. The statements often used for the nurturing adult to offer to the wounded child are, "You're

okay now. I've got you. I won't let them hurt you anymore.
I love you. You are my precious child, and I'm here for
you. You can count on me." These self-nurturing statements are usually well received, and an effective integration with the inner child can be facilitated.

Sometimes, however, the patient will go back into fear,
or will flash to another abusive memory. This is simply an
indication that there is more work to be done. It does not
detract from the significance of the healing which has
occurred up to that point.

AN EXPERIENCE OF BEING
WHOLE AND COMPLETE

The goal of healing and therapeutic work is to become
whole. This is accomplished emotionally through the integration of the current adult with the wounded child of the
past. The current adult, in the form of a nurturing strong
parent, goes to the wounded child in times of need as
presented by the subconscious mind in the form of visual
and verbal memory. New awareness of the child's basic
innocence and need for love is the motivation for the
nurturing parent. Strength is derived from the experience
of healthy appropriate anger, directed at the injustice of
what happened to the child.

As the adult becomes stronger in the role of the nurturing parent, that adult goes to each painful memory with
strength, love and healing for the wounded child. Before
this, the wounded child had been emotionally frozen at
the points of trauma. Through the healing process, the
child is set free from these trauma points to allow full and
complete emotional energy to move into present adult
experiences. This allows for the development of emotional
maturity. This is a primary foundation for personal spiritual wholeness.

I have all that I need to be whole and complete.
My anger is my ally in my journey past fear and
*   pain.*
My feelings live in my body and I am open to all that
*   I feel.*
All of my memories are here for my healing and
*   growth.*
My subconscious mind provides me with all the
information I need in order to become whole and
*   complete.*
I am open to all that my mind offers me.
I am open to all that life offers me.

10

Managing And Expressing Anger In Adult Relationships

HOW ABOUT A NICE KISS!?

NICE KISS! is a mnemonic device I use to teach and remember a simple process for identifying and expressing feelings. This only works when a person has done most of their own basic healing and recovery work. No simple "how to" process is going to be effective for someone who has primary unresolved issues. This chapter is for those who have made significant progress in their own growth and healing and are ready to begin communicating their feelings in adult relationships.

Here's how the NICE KISS! works:

Notice the feeling
Identify the feeling
Claim the feeling
Express the feeling

Keep
It
Simple,
Sweetheart!

Now I will elaborate on the intimate details of this NICE KISS!:

Notice the feeling. Ask your stomach, your heart, your chest, your neck, your shoulders, your back and even your head (if you have headaches) what you are feeling. Don't expect the answer to be in your brain. Your brain will give you silly answers like, "I don't feel anything," or "I think I feel . . ." or "I feel confused." (Confusion is in our thinking. It's not a feeling.) Right now, ask the part of your body where you carry your stress to tell you how you are feeling. Before putting the answer into words though, wait until you finish your NICE KISS!

Identify the feeling. To do this, you want to start applying your KISS! (Keep It Simple, Sweetheart). One of the ways we get out and stay out of touch with our feelings is by being too "headsy" and abstract in the words we use to describe them. By using simple clear words, we express more feeling in the process of speaking the word.

Try choosing from the feeling words used in the concentric circle diagram. That gives you *anger, fear, pain, hurt, love,* and *need for love* as options for feeling words. If none of these fit, but you know the feeling is not a positive one, see if the word you would use to describe your feeling might be a part of fear, pain or a need for love. Lonely, for example, is definitely a need for love. Anxious, tense and stressed out are all abstractions of anger, fear and pain. If you are having a positive feeling, let's assume it fits in the center with the need to love and be loved.

Claim the feeling. This is as opposed to blaming the feeling on someone else. One of the best ways I know to do this is to imagine your inner child having the feeling. That is, picture your inner child hurting, afraid, joyful, lovable or in need of love. If anger is the feeling you identify, try to find the fear or pain that is beneath it. Claim the anger as a protective feeling, felt by the nurturing parent for your hurt or frightened inner child. Next, pick up and embrace your inner child, feeling the deeper, more vulnerable feelings within yourself. Allow the child to move into your heart, which is its home. The feeling is yours, you have claimed it. You're in charge.

Express the feeling. Everything up to this point has been an internal, private process. Now it's time to talk about your feelings to someone else.

There are two basic reasons to talk about your feelings. One reason is because it is healthy for you. Suppressing feelings is unhealthy, expressing them is healthy. You are expressing your feelings for yourself, not for an expected result. You have no idea what the result will be, and there are no guarantees that it will be received in the way you want it to be. To suppress your feelings is to deny your worth and value as a person. You are past that now. Part of your commitment to yourself is to express your feelings in a healthy manner, in an environment which is as appropriate and safe as possible. Another reason is for the purpose of making a connection with another person. Intimacy is established through honest open communication of feelings. Again you are not looking for results, you are just doing your part of allowing for intimacy by expressing your feelings. This is where it becomes particularly important to keep it simple, sweetheart.

IT ALL BOILS DOWN TO LOVE

We are most likely to have intense feelings, including anger, in our more intimate relationships where there is more need to give and receive love. The more we love someone, the more vulnerable to being hurt we are and the deeper the pain when we are hurt. This is not bad or a problem to be solved — it's just the way it is. Because the pain is greater (at least potentially), the fear is usually greater also. Thus it follows that the anger in intimate close relationships is more intense than in casual relationships in which there is less love, pain and fear. As we have already mentioned, there is more violence in the home than in any other sector. My belief is that the violence springs from the anger which ultimately springs from a tremendous need to love and be loved.

There is, fortunately, a level of emotional maturity we can reach where our intimate relationships do not contain much pain, fear or anger. Most of us are still working toward that goal. So the more love there is, the more potential we have for pain, fear and anger. It is also true that the more love there is, the more potential we have for resolution of pain, fear and anger.

EXPRESS YOUR FEELINGS FOR YOU, NOT FOR RESULTS

The point has been well made that suppressing feelings is hazardous to our health. It is also clear that expressing them in appropriate ways is healthy. For this reason it doesn't make sense to only express our feelings if we think the listener wants to hear them. Many times the listener will not want to hear our feelings. They are usually too full of their own to be able to clearly receive what we are offering. So we have to do it for us! Timing is important, however. I will elaborate on that further at a later point.

If we are looking for certain results when we decide to express our feelings, we will usually be disappointed. It takes a really healthy person to be truly open to hearing about your pain, fear and anger. You may find it just as rare for someone to be open to hearing about your joy and excitement.

One of the most common statements I hear in my practice when I encourage people to express their feelings to their loved ones is, "I tried that and they . . ." Get the picture? In other words, we try this business of being open with our feelings and telling our loved ones what's really going on and they just don't act right. So we give up and go back to suppressing our feelings and being depressed, constantly angry, passive aggressive or periodically explosive. The material in Chapter 5 dealing with creating healthy boundaries and commitment priorities may be helpful here.

I often tell my clients to preface expression of their feelings with any combination of the following statements:

"I don't want you to fix me or give me any advice. I'm not trying to change or fix you. I just want you to listen to me and be here. You don't even have to say anything if you don't want to. I am telling you about my feelings because they are an important part of who I am, and it's good for me to express them."

This doesn't guarantee any results, but if the other person is paying attention and is fairly clear with their own issues, it could help to create a productive interaction. If the other person responds well and the relationship benefits, great. If the relationship can't ultimately handle your being open with your feelings, it is not a healthy relationship for you. Remember, you are doing this for yourself. Our feelings are who we are inside. To deny them is to deny ourselves. To express them is to accept and love ourselves and to claim responsibility for who we are. When there is no more shame, there is no more reason to hide our feelings.

MAKING THE CONNECTION

Since our basic emotional need is to love and be loved, it follows that we need to make connections with those who are important to us. Expressing feelings is essential to this process. Most of us have believed that if we can only please the other person, they will love us, everything will be fine and all these feelings will just go away. With these expectations, we have probably had several failed relationships. Perhaps we learned about co-dependency and decided we didn't want to live like that any more. Now it is time to get down to the business of learning to build and maintain healthy adult relationships based on openness, honesty and mutual respect. With these ingredients, and some love and basic skills thrown in, all we need is persistence.

It is important to point out the difference between trying to connect with the other person and going for results. This is a very subtle distinction. If there were not some desire to connect, we could express our feelings to a cup of coffee. Here's the difference between trying to connect and going for results.

When going for results, we are trying to get the other person to do something or to respond in some particular way. This can only lead to disappointment and misery. When connection is the goal, we are simply offering our expression to the other person in the way we feel they will be most likely to receive it. That's all we do. We are offering ourselves. What the other person does is their own business. When this offering is made with no expectations or demands, the other person is free to respond in the way that is best for them in that moment. If we truly love and respect them, that is what we want.

The Journey From Me To You

My words stumble and stagger
On their way from garble
To meaning

On their way from in here
To you
Out there, listening.

Why is it so far
From my feelings
Through my thoughts
To your mind?

Why do I try so hard
To reach you
Who seem so far away?

Aahh, yes
The connection . . .

Your eyes are sparkling
Our souls have touched

It was well worth the journey.

I wrote this poem while contemplating this very subject of connection. It is a difficult journey at times, but the rewards of true connection cause us to embark again and again.

Let's consider some guidelines that seem to work for making the journey as smooth and effective as possible.

Being current. This only means expressing those feelings while they are fresh. Being current with your feelings is as much for your own sake as for the other person. Suppressed feelings hurt the suppressor. Old, suppressed feelings are no fun to hear about when they come out. Support groups or therapy may be the best place to let out the suppressed feelings so you can be current and fresh with the people you care about the most.

Being clear. This goes back to the NICE KISS! Use words that are easily understood by the listener. Get clear within yourself before trying to connect emotionally with another person. Look at the concentric circles of emotion in Figure 5.1, and move from the outer circles into the center. In other words:

1. Use your skill, strength and knowledge to take down the defenses by talking about them. "I'm very angry right now, and I feel like leaving" (anger and withdrawal). "But instead of doing that, I'm going to tell you how I feel." You may want to use the prefacing statements described above in the *Express Your Feelings For You, Not For Results* section.

2. Talk about the fear you are feeling. "When this happens, I tell myself that things will never change and it

will be like this forever. I'm afraid that everything will just get worse, and you will leave or I will leave or we will stay together and be miserable. In the past I have always tried to fix or change you at this point, but now I am just telling you how I feel."

You've taken down the defenses and now you are being vulnerable, which is a sign of strength and maturity. You might also talk about the other kind of fear, the one we call shame. "I'm also afraid that it's all my fault and I'm screwing this up just like I have everything else. I feel like I am bad, and that's why the bad things keep happening. I know in my head it's not true, but that's what I feel." Shame lives in the shadows. Bring it out into the light of day, and it is not so powerful as it once seemed to be. It might just go away.

3. Talk about your pain. Now you are really showing a commitment to the journey. You are getting closer to the heart of the matter, the center of the circle. "I'm really hurting right now. This feels just like those times in my childhood when I was hurt or rejected. I can handle my pain, but I want you to know what's going on with me." (This is always a good time to reassure the other person that you don't need them to fix you.) "I don't want you to do anything, just hear me."

You are now showing trust — of yourself primarily. This is an important point. Ultimately as we learn to trust ourselves, we are better able to trust that we will be safe with others. This sharing of pain and hurt should only be done when you feel confident that you can take care of yourself, no matter how the other person responds. They may simply not be able to support you. They may even attack you out of their own fear. They may be hurting so much themselves that they can't talk. That's why you have to do it for yourself, just in case the other person has nothing to offer you in that moment.

4. Talk about the love. If you don't feel like using the word "love" in such a moment when you are feeling angry, hurt and afraid, tell the other person you are doing all this because they are important to you. If they were not im-

portant to you, you would not be having all these feelings. "I'm telling you all of this instead of leaving or trying to drive you away because you and this relationship are important to me. I care about you, and I want this relationship to last. I don't want to hurt you. I do want you to understand me, because that helps me to relax and be myself in your presence." Or if it fits, you may be more intimate with a statement like, "I love you. I want you to love me. This is the most important relationship in my life. I want you to know how I feel inside because I want to be close to you, to feel connected."

Being sensitive. This is a matter of paying attention to timing. Being sensitive in this context also involves being aware and using your intelligence. Expressing your feelings effectively does not mean letting your feelings be in charge. Our thoughts need to be in charge so we can make decisions and act on them. This is also essential if we are to be sensitive to the important element of timing in communication. If you have been at home all day or evening building up a plan for telling your spouse how you feel, it may not be wise to lay it all on them when they walk in the door. To ignore the importance of timing is to set yourself up for failure and sabotage your own success in communication.

We also have to be careful about the other extreme. I have often heard the statement, "There just never seemed to be a good time to discuss these things." That can be a defense against the fear of risking in open communication. Somewhere in the middle of these two extremes is a time that may not be perfect, but is the best we have to choose from for now. Here are some points to consider in timing of feelings expression:

- Late at night is usually not the best time. It may be your only time, however, and talking about your feelings then is better than not talking about them at all.
- Family members of drug addicts and alcoholics usually know it is useless to talk to the addicted person during a using binge or while their system is highly toxic. If

there are no periods of relative sobriety, it may be time for an intervention, which can include many of the expressions of feelings outlined above.

- When the other person is hungry, angry, tired or generally stressed out, you are not likely to be received. You may want to schedule a time to be with your significant other when you know they are most likely to be open and receptive.

- When the feelings between you are fairly pleasant and relaxed, it may be a good time to share your emotions in an intimate way. A risk here is that you may think, "This feels good. I don't want to spoil it by talking about all those yucky feelings. I'll wait until later." The problem is that later will not be good either, for the reasons we have discussed. This is one of the ways we keep ourselves stuck and never express our feelings until something makes us explode.

- Sometimes we just have to pick a time and go for it. If you can't find what appears to be a good time, do it anyway.

Being responsible for yourself. Remember, you are not doing this to change the other person. (You might want to review the prefacing statements outlined above. It is interesting that the word "prefacing" broken down is prefacing, implying something you do before facing someone with your feelings.) You are expressing your feelings because it is healthy for you to do so. You are in the process of learning to love yourself and doing what is healthy is a big part of loving yourself.

This means that if the other person doesn't respond the way you want them to, you still know what to do. This is when your skills for self-nurturing need to kick in. You didn't get the support you needed, so you give some support to yourself. Your words to your inner child may be something like, "I love you, no matter what they say or do. I think you are wonderful, and you are the best part of me. You are my precious child, and it's okay for you to feel anything you want. I love you right now, while you are hurting and scared. I'm angry because you have been hurt, but I won't let my anger make things worse. My anger is for your protection, and that's how I am using it. I'll keep you safe, and we won't try talking to them again until you feel secure. You are my top priority, and you can count on me."

Taking responsibility in this way prevents blaming or attacking the other for their insensitivity. Blame and attack puts you in the victim role and only adds to your pain and fear. If you find you are filled with anger or even rage, you may be comfortable using some of the anger release methods described earlier. If you are not or this doesn't seem to work for you, you may want to find a therapist who does this type of work and schedule a session. The point is to notice, identify, claim and express (NICE KISS!) your feelings — without blaming or attacking anyone and without hurting yourself.

You deserve support and love, so if you don't get it from the other person, give it to yourself. This is also a good time for returning to a spiritual focus, which is a source of support and love that is unconditional and unlimited. Sometimes loving yourself in the form of nurturing your inner child opens the door to your heart and allows spiritual love to enter, however you may define this for yourself.

KNOW WHEN TO WALK AWAY

Part of being responsible includes being sensitive to our own needs and feelings. We need to know when our emotions are just too intense for us to try to communicate. We need to know when to withdraw in a healthy way. This does not mean emotional withdrawal, where we shut down and try to act as if everything is okay when it's not. What we're talking about here is physical withdrawal to another part of the house, outdoors to take a walk or even taking a break for a few days or weeks to become emotionally and intellectually integrated enough to communicate effectively.

Here are some examples of situations that might require a period of healthy withdrawal:

1. You can't think straight. No matter what you try, you are just not getting your point across.
2. You are so emotional you feel you are going to explode or you can't stop yelling or crying. You're stuck in a pattern of arguing or blaming. It's time to nurture and care for yourself. Staying with the other person is not going to help unless they just happen to be very healthy, balanced and skilled in helping you through such intense emotions.
3. Physical or emotional abuse is occurring. Leave the situation immediately. You know that it is only going to get worse before it gets better. By withdrawing in a healthy way, you are saying, "I deserve better treatment than this, and I will not stay in a situation where I am being abused." If you are the one who is doing the abusing, it is essential that you stop the abuse and withdraw yourself in a healthy way. Perpetrators of abuse are hurting themselves as well as their victims.
4. During periods of illness, withdrawal from interaction with others is sometimes helpful so we can listen to what our bodies are telling us. Illness and pain can be great teachers if we allow them to be. Our bodies have great wisdom which comes only in silent still moments without distraction.
5. Sometimes withdrawal is important even if there are no major problems. Healthy intimate relationships involve a movement like breathing, which allows an open expansive period in which the connection is the top priority, followed by a more closed, distant period when one or both people are more focused within. Withdrawal from intimate communication is essential to allow for centering and self-nurturing. Another way of saying this is that in order to maintain our friendship with ourselves, we must spend some time alone. When we are alone,

we get in touch with feelings which are otherwise not as noticeable because of the distractions provided by the other people present.

Here are some statements we might make in withdrawing from communication with another person:

- "I'm not happy with the way I am communicating with you right now. I need some time to figure out what I am feeling and what I need to do about those feelings. I will talk with you some more about it this afternoon." (Or tomorrow, next week or when you're ready — whatever is appropriate to the circumstances. It is important that you get back with the person so your withdrawal doesn't just seem like some form of punishment.)
- "I deserve to be treated with respect and so do you. Neither of us is doing that right now. I am taking a break to figure out my feelings and my needs. I will talk to you when I figure out what I want to communicate to you."
- "I haven't been feeling well lately. I don't think it is just a simple illness, and I don't think I am a victim of some outside force. I need to find out what my responsibility is for what's going on in my life, and I need some time alone to do that."

Sometimes you just have to leave. You may be in such a state that you can't think of anything to say that you have not already said, and it is time for action. This may be the healthiest option in some situations.

The other person will often feel rejected, hurt or angry when you do this or make any of the above statements. Respect them enough to let them have their own pain, fear and anger. You simply can't fix them or how they are feeling. They may try to stop you or make you feel guilty, out of their own fear of abandonment. You may or may not want to reassure them that it is not their fault, depending on the health of the relationship. If you let them convince you not to take care of yourself in this way, you

are simply contributing to your problems and to the problems of the relationship.

Healthy withdrawal is a very clear message to yourself.
The message is, "I deserve my own attention. It is time
for me to give some quiet, focused attention to my own
feelings and needs. I have nothing to fear within myself.
I am a friend to myself, and I am now choosing to spend
some time with my friend."

THE REWARD

Expressing your feelings in healthy ways will help. If
there are no major unaddressed or unresolved issues from
your past, using the guidelines set out in this book should
work for you. If you have not done any healing work
regarding your own childhood, these methods may only
create new problems. There are no quick fixes or easy
answers. You can, however, reach your goals for health
and happiness if you set your mind to it and use all of
your available resources.

Close, warm, intimate relationships are fantastic. The
feeling of true connection with another person is well
worth the journey. It seems to me that developing close
intimate relationships is one of the most challenging and
rewarding frontiers of personal growth. It also seems
when I see or feel the essence of a truly healthy, loving
relationship, that it may be one of the highest forms of
human experience. The love that can grow in a deep commitment between two healthy individuals is a fulfilling,
uplifting and healing experience. It is my further belief
that an essential ingredient in such a relationship is a spiritual focus of some kind. This prevents us from making
gods and goddesses out of our loved ones, attaching great
expectations to their behavior and their ability to make
our lives wonderful. We can make our own lives wonderful.
Then when we come together with someone who is doing
the same thing, the results are uplifting and fulfilling.

I am responsible for my feelings in each of my relationships.

My first commitment is to myself, then to my role in the relationship and finally to the relationship itself.

The only connection for which I have full responsibility is my emotional and spiritual connection with myself.

11

Expanding The Circle From Within

Looking back over the various diagrams presented in earlier chapters, you will find that the innermost circles of the concentric circle diagrams contain the need to love and be loved, a commitment to self, the inner child and a spiritual focus point. Ultimately healing involves an expansion of these inner dimensions, so that our most innocent and loving self becomes the predominant aspect of who we are. Everything presented in this book has been leading toward an expansion of love and healing from within. This is the function of expressing emotions in healthy ways.

THE INNER JOURNEY OF HEALING

The journey begins with an increase in skill, knowledge, strength and awareness, not of the world outside, but of the world within ourselves. This is the outer circle, the place we live in our conscious minds most of the time. The first leg of our journey is to identify and diffuse our own defenses. We have to make sure that our childhood defenses don't prevent our adult growth and development. The realm of defense and protection can cut us off from our own feelings if we let it.

By becoming aware and taking charge of this aspect of our self-protection, we are making it our ally instead of an obstacle. This is where we pick up the energy of anger for facing the next dimension. We might see Figure 11.1 as representing a road map for the journey within. We have just left the outer circle and are gaining power in the circle of protection to face the wall of fear.

Empowered by anger at the injustice of our childhood injuries, we break through the wall of fear and encounter the inner realms of hurt, sorrow and pain. The healthy anger we have gained as an ally is based on compassion for the wounded child. When we contact the pain of the child, we automatically feel love for this innocent being, who has been abused, neglected or abandoned by adult caregivers. This is where the journey always leads. The more we make this journey, the more healing occurs and the more the wall of fear and the realm of pain diminish. Each time we contact the inner circle of love for the inner child, it expands, dissolving the pain and fear. Eventually the inner world begins to transform entirely.

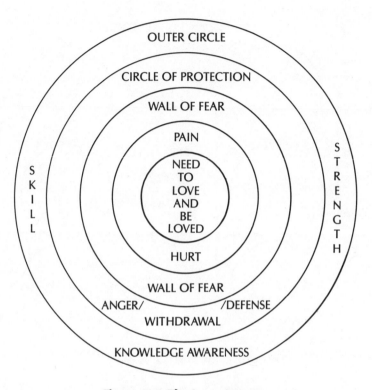

Figure 11.1. The Inner Journey

PERSONAL INTEGRATION AND INTEGRITY

As a part of healing, we must master the art of living a healthy balanced life. This is no small task, and it demands that we use all that we have and all that we are to succeed. One way of looking at who we are as human beings is to think of us as an integrated system of thought, action and feeling. In the diagram in Figure 11.2 you will see that thought, action and feeling are analogous to the parent, adult and child relationships.

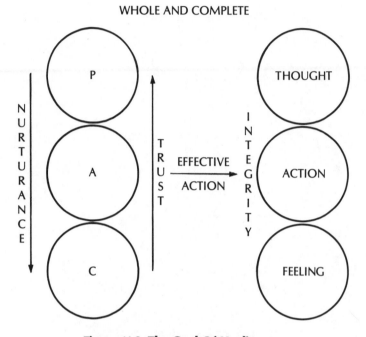

Figure 11.2. The Goal Of Healing

As the nurturing parent provides protection, support and love for the inner child, the inner child begins to trust the nurturing parent. This was illustrated in Chapter 6, in the dialogues with the inner child. This, of course, makes the adult more effective, with all of the internal resources working together. In the same way as our thoughts about ourselves become more positive, we will begin to feel more secure and our actions will become more powerful and focused. If you look at the two sets of three circles in Figure 11.2, you can see how this works.

It follows that nurturing our inner child is a way of more effectively integrating our thoughts, actions and feelings. By the same token, thinking positive thoughts about our feelings is a way of nurturing our inner child. The more internally integrated we are in our thoughts, actions and feelings, the more integrity we will demonstrate in our relationships with others. We might summarize with the statement that our relationships with others reflect our relationship with ourselves.

To effectively take charge of our thoughts, actions and feelings, we must examine what patterns and habits already exist. One of the best ways to do this is to take a look at our family of origin and examine the messages we received there. Figure 11.3 shows a way of identifying some of those messages and how they affected us. As you can see in the diagram, the spoken words we heard as children affect our thoughts of today. The behavior we observed in our parents to a large extent determines our actions today. The most subtle influence our parents had on us was emotional. We were picking up on feelings even before we came out of our mother's womb. The emotions we perceived from our parents had a profound subconscious effect on how we feel about ourselves and our world today.

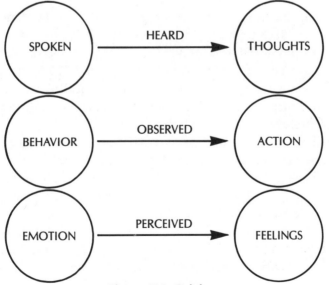

Figure 11.3. Origins

UNLOADING FAMILY BAGGAGE

From the points made throughout this book and from your own life experience, you probably know the value of resolving issues relating to your family of origin. We must each examine the thoughts, actions and feelings we subconsciously soaked up during our formative years at home.

Much of what you learned was useful or you would not have the intelligence and skill to read this book. It is just as important to recognize what you received that was valuable as it is to unload what you don't need anymore. If you don't acknowledge the gifts, you may feel guilty in the process of identifying the baggage you want to unload. Take an inventory of what you picked up. Separate out what you want to keep and what you want to give back. Be grateful for what you got that is useful. Return to your parents what you received that is getting in the way of your being the person you want to be. They never meant to pass on their hang-ups to you anyway. Taking them back is no hardship on them, because they never really gave them up in the first place.

(By the way, I am not implying that this be done in person, face to face with your parents. They neither need to be physically present nor even living for you to resolve these issues for yourself. It may be helpful to involve them in your healing process if they are healthy and ready to participate. Otherwise, you may be adding to existing problems instead of unloading baggage.)

This business of "giving back" unwanted baggage to your parents may sound strange to you but it really is possible. It usually is done in a therapeutic context in which Gestalt techniques are employed to create a valid emotional release from abusive and shaming childhood experiences. There are also workbooks available such as Dr. Charles Whitfield's *A Gift To Myself*, which is designed to help with the process of healing the inner child. John Bradshaw's *Homecoming* is also designed for this purpose. These workbooks often include exercises for resolving family-of-origin issues, along with the other healing and affirmation methods.

As a result of this inner healing work, walls begin to disappear, and we become more clear and open to ourselves and to the world around us.

A DYNAMIC BREATHING SYSTEM

In comparing the diagrams in Figure 11.4 with those in Figure 11.1, you can see that the inner and outer circles have expanded until they connected, removing the walls of fear and pain. You will also notice that the system is an open one, indicated by the broken lines in the top diagram. This allows more expression of love and joy in relationship to the world. It also allows for more receptivity to input from others. This is a flexible, breathing system of healthy boundaries.

In the diagram on the bottom of Figure 11.4, there is more protection and more privacy from the world. We each need this for self-nurturing, rest and spiritual focusing. When we are rejuvenated and ready, we open to the world again, expressing and receiving openly as in the top diagram. This is my idea of how we maintain our health and happiness in a demanding and changing world. We have times when we are open and expansive and times when we are quiet and private, more focused within. This is as natural as breathing in and breathing out.

As discussed in the preceding chapter, we each need the opportunity to be close and intimate with others, while maintaining responsibility for our own needs and feelings. With the flexibility indicated in the opening and closing pattern of Figure 11.4, we can give and receive nurturing in a close relationship without being dependent on the other. We can also withdraw and have time to ourselves as needed without being isolated. While in the open mode, we may express our anger, fear and pain (yes, it is still there, but it is not like it used to be) without losing touch with love and compassion. The backlog of pain, fear

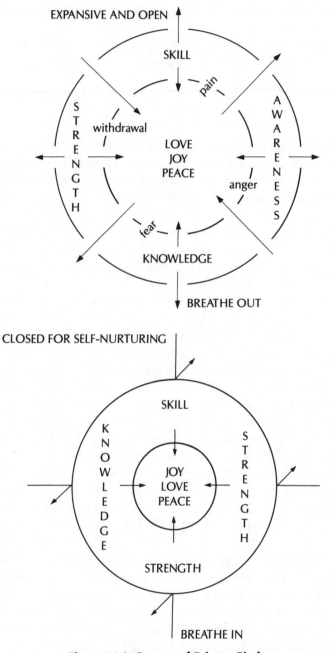

Figure 11.4. Open and Private Circles

and anger from the past has been healed so the current emotions are manageable and can be easily communicated. From a clear, healthy place, the simple expression of feelings clears the emotion. Connections are easily made and they are not threatening. This is the rest of the establishment and maintenance of healthy, flexible boundaries.

THE HEALTHY ADULT RELATIONSHIP

For more perspective on how this dynamic system might work in a healthy adult relationship, take a look at the diagram in Figure 11.5. Both individuals represented have a nurturing, trusting relationship with themselves. Therefore, there is internal stability and balance within both people, allowing for free expression of intimacy at all levels. As indicated by the arrow connecting the two sides at the adult level, the primary connection is adult to adult.

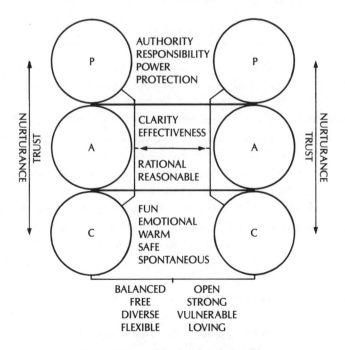

Figure 11.5. Healthy Adult Relationship

The two are, however, able to communicate at the level of authority and responsibility, which is needed for raising children or taking charge of any demanding situation, such as paying bills or solving problems. Because of their personal freedom and flexibility, however, they can also connect emotionally at the child level. This is essential if there is going to be fun, spontaneity or lovemaking in the relationship.

Both individuals must be healthy in order to freely allow the true intimacy and healthy withdrawal necessary for a healthy adult relationship. This dynamic breathing system gives those involved an opportunity to grow and develop as they are compelled to from within. This type of relationship is an enhancement to the lives of everyone involved. It is my belief that this is the type of relationship that each of us truly desires.

SKILLS FOR BEING FULLY PRESENT

To the extent that we are being subconsciously influenced by our past, we are not fully present in any relationship. To the extent that we have resolved past issues, we are capable of thinking, acting and feeling completely within the present moment. This is when we are most effective and most likely to act in ways consistent with our thoughts and feelings. This results in personal integrity as we discussed earlier in this chapter.

Most of the time we are thinking about one thing, doing something else and completely unaware of our feelings. This disjointed or disintegrated way of being leads to tension and stress because we are actually in conflict with ourselves. We are most likely to have accidents or make costly mistakes when we are out of "sync" in this way. It follows that once the influences of the past have been released, it would be very much to our advantage to take conscious control of our thoughts, actions and feelings in a positive manner.

In Figure 11.6, you will see three different skill group-
ings, one each for thoughts, actions and feelings.

Affirmation.

All of our lives we have had different thoughts and
beliefs affirmed by those around us. Our first thoughts
were greatly influenced by our parents. As we moved out
into the world, the influences were our peers, teachers
and the media. This set of skills is simply designed to help
you be an influence on your own thoughts, rather than
accepting uncritically the constant influence of the world
around you. We are always affirming something in our
minds as a natural function of our thinking process. You
may have heard the aphorism, "You are today what your
thoughts were yesterday. You will be tomorrow what your
thoughts are today."

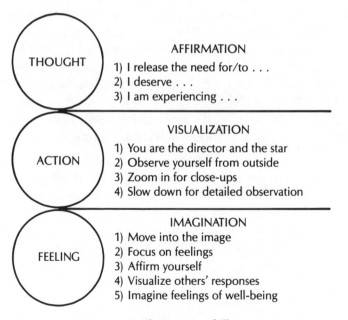

Figure 11.6. Skills

As you can see in Figure 11.6, there are three levels of affirmation. The first deals with the past, the second with the present and the third affirms the new action or experience in the future. I will use one example throughout the skills exercise to provide continuity and to demonstrate how each of these skills can be applied in conjunction to one specific problem or change area.

1. I release the need for/to . . . (feel like a victim in my relationships).
2. I deserve . . . (to feel empowered and comfortable with myself in all of my relationships).
3. I am experiencing . . . (more of a sense of comfort and empowerment within myself as each new day unfolds).

Affirmations often stir up major objections from our conscious and subconscious mind, in the form of negative and fearful thoughts. These self-defeating thoughts are coming from a frightened part of us. They are not bad or something to be resisted. When this occurs, simply embrace your inner child and say, "It's okay to feel afraid. I've got you, and I will take care of you through all of these new changes." Then go back to the thoughts. You don't want to let the fearful mind get the last word. Here are a fourth and fifth level of the affirmation exercise that are helpful for responding to self-defeating thoughts.

4. Negative or contradictory thoughts which arose are . . . (Every time I try to stand up for myself, I get hurt or something bad happens. Besides, I'm afraid of changing. I've always been like this.)
5. Thoughts in response to the negative or contradictory thoughts are . . . (It's okay to be afraid. I'm also angry about the way my life is going, and I am determined to use my anger to empower me to make positive changes. I am experiencing a sense of empowerment within myself right now as I think of my healthy anger and how it can help me move out of the victim position.)

This same exercise can be used to address a wide variety of areas in your life. You will find a copy of the *Affirmations Exercise* in the Appendix in the back of this book, which you are free to copy and use for your own growth and development. You will find "target areas" listed in this exercise, which are merely suggestions as to how you might focus your affirmations work.

Louise Hay's book, *You Can Heal Your Life*, and Ruth Fishel's *The Journey Within: A Spiritual Path To Recovery* are excellent resources for affirmation work.

As a final note in this section, I would like to say that as human beings we can do anything we set our minds to. Decide what you want and go for it.

Visualization.

Have you ever heard anyone say, "I just can't picture myself doing that"? When we hear statements like that, we know for sure the person is not going to do what they can't picture themselves doing. It also follows that if we can picture ourselves doing something, we are much more likely to do it. This exercise is just that simple. If you want to do something, picture yourself doing it.

1. You are the director and the star. This means you are picturing yourself out there in front of you, engaging in your new behavior. It's as if you were both the director and the star on a movie set.

2. Observe yourself from the outside, from the director's position. You are concerned with how you, the actor, are presenting yourself. To continue with our example from the affirmation section, picture yourself in a situation where you have historically felt uncomfortable and anxious, like a victim of your circumstances. This time, however, you are seeing yourself as you would like to be, calm and confident. Notice how you look from across the room. Look for indicators that you are completely at ease.

3. Now move in more closely and notice how deep and even your breathing is. Your skin shows a glow that

indicates good circulation and relaxed muscles. There's a sparkle in your eyes, and you look as if you are right where you are supposed to be. To help with this image, you may want to picture yourself in a situation where it is easy for you to feel relaxed, and then move that image into the challenging situation.

4. Slow the action for a moment and watch yourself as you move about, interacting with others. Notice how you present yourself pleasantly and with confidence. Your head is up and you are looking directly into the eyes of the other person. You are showing a sincere interest in them while remaining centered and focused within yourself.

Remember to stay on the outside throughout the visualization exercise, so your focus is on your behavior. When you have successfully accomplished your goal of seeing yourself as you would like to be, it's time to bring the image in, and to *imag(e)in(e)* having the feelings you have been picturing yourself having.

Imagination.
This is where you begin to come closer to actually having the experience. You rise from the director's chair and walk across the room.

1. Move into the image of the star (bring the image in). The director and the star are now one, and you are in the situation. You are now seeing what the star was seeing during your visualization exercise.
2. Focus on the feelings. Don't allow yourself to be distracted by what you are seeing in the room around you. Be aware of what is present while maintaining focus on your own bodily sensations of warmth, relaxation and comfort. Notice your breathing. You are breathing from your stomach in long, deep inhalations and exhalations. This is happening naturally with no effort on your part. Notice the relaxed energetic feelings in your body. You can feel the pleas-

ant sensations in your body moving up into your face, creating a pleasant calm expression.

3. Affirm yourself. Use some of the affirmations from the exercise above, or create new ones to repeat to yourself as you imagine yourself calm and at ease. Tell yourself exactly what you would like to hear. Give yourself the support you have always wanted. Be your own best friend and supporter.

4. Visualize others' responses. Picture the other person in front of you. They may be uncomfortable with your new sense of confidence and ease. They also may be very positive in their response. Imagine yourself being completely okay with their response whatever it may be. They may try to pull you back into old patterns so they can be more comfortable since that is what they are used to. Still you stay relaxed while focusing on the pleasant, soothing feelings of calm moving throughout your body and face. If they persist with attempts to pull you off center, simply imagine yourself calmly announcing that you have other things to do and you will reconnect with them at another time. You may want to go back to the visualization exercise to begin this process of leaving the situation with comfort and ease. You may also want to imagine yourself expressing your feelings in a new way.

5. Imagine feelings of well-being. Notice a feeling of stillness deep within your being. There is a silence in the center of your mind, which seems to arise from this stillness. In that silence, you find that the words you need to say are spontaneously emerging. From the stillness, you find that the feelings you want to have spontaneously arise. Words that seem to go with these feelings of well-being are comfortable, easy, relaxed, confident, calm, empowered, energetic, peaceful, focused, centered and still. Use these words to create new affirmations for yourself to apply to your life in general as well as specific situations in which you would like to improve yourself.

By taking charge of your own thoughts, actions and feelings, you are directing a tremendous amount of energy into the core of your being. This will bring an inevitable expansion of your sense of self-worth and value. You will no longer feel fragmented and incomplete. Maybe this is what is meant by "getting it together."

EXPERIENCE BEING WHOLE AND COMPLETE

While reading through the above exercises, whether you actually applied the exercises to a situation from your life or not, you probably felt some of the feelings being described. The mere process of thinking of the words *comfort* and *ease* requires our mind to recall their meaning. As we recall the meaning of these words, our subconscious mind is busy providing examples from our past when we in fact knew the meaning of comfort and ease. As this process unfolds, sometimes in a split second, some degree of comfort and ease actually begins to occur within our bodies.

Body, mind and emotion are not separate, but intricately interwoven in ways we have only begun to understand. As we make affirming statements to ourselves and think of soothing, empowering words, our emotional body is responding, whether we know it consciously or not. When we picture ourselves in our mind's eye as successful and confident, behaving in ways we are completely comfortable with, our body responds with the appropriate feelings. When we imagine ourselves as actually having the experience we want to have, we are actually having the experience we want to have.

Regardless of what happens in your daily life, practicing these exercises will increase your feelings of well-being and ease. They are designed to give you power and control within yourself, which you are actually exercising by affirming, visualizing and imagining.

When your thoughts, actions and feelings are working together in ways you have chosen for your health and well-being, you are acting in an integrated manner. You are fully present, and your whole being is completely involved in each element of each experience in each moment. This is what we are here for. This is how we maximize our individual expression of this miraculous gift of life that we are.

I can do anything I set my mind to.
I have a brilliant mind.
I release the need to limit my mind in any way.
I deserve to be the best me I can possibly be.
I am experiencing more of my true essential self with each new day.
I am becoming familiar with a place of stillness and peace within my being.
When I relax and focus on the silence within my mind, answers to questions and solutions to problems spontaneously arise.
My natural state of being is one of comfort and ease.
I have everything I need to be whole and complete.

12

Conclusions And Brainstorms

THE END OF THE VICTIM ROLE

Imagine with me for a moment what the world would be like if no one ever felt like a victim. This would be a world in which people took responsibility for their feelings and for the situations they found themselves in. Without the victim position, there would be no "bad guy" out there to blame for our circumstances. In this world we would feel empowered from within. When something didn't go our way, we would work through the emotional reactions and then get busy doing what we could to make the situation better. It would not be a perfect world, but it would have much more positive action and much less complaining and self-pity. There would be fewer addictive disorders, since many of these arise from a feeling of helplessness and despair. Helplessness and despair arise from feeling like a victim.

This is why I believe this matter of claiming our power through claiming our anger as a healthy emotion is so important. Experiencing and expressing anger in healthy ways is a first step toward moving out of the victim position. We cannot feel angry — with the full physical components of heat, adrenaline and energy — and feel like a victim at the same time.

Granted, feeling like a victim often gives rise to anger. The problem is that anger coming from a victim position usually goes into blaming, attacking or even hating the persecutor. As I have discussed in previous chapters, this is a phase of healing for those who were indeed victimized in the past. It is not a goal, however. Anger for empowerment comes from a sense of what is right and just, and is used only to heal and to creatively express.

A world in which no one felt like a victim would be a world of empowerment, freedom and responsibility. This world would have more joy and fulfillment, simply because more people would reach their goals and live their dreams. This world would have more love and less fear, since removing victim feelings would also remove a tremendous amount of fear. Fear and love are incompatible. An absence of fear would automatically give rise to more love.

SOCIOLOGICAL AND PLANETARY PERSPECTIVE

The patterns of oppression, suppression and rage are clear and prevalent in our society and throughout the world. Slavery is one of the greatest oppressions known to humankind. Slaves had to suppress their emotions to prevent their oppression from getting worse. Expressing their emotions may even have meant being tortured and killed.

Rage is one of the maladies that always results from oppression and suppression. It makes sense that slavery brought out rage within the people who were oppressed. This is a natural human response to such treatment.

The Civil War in the United States is an example of a nation raging against itself. The Civil Rights movement involved some rage but also the use of healthy anger.

Oppression and abuse of African-Americans today have brought further emotional suppression and more rage. This has continued long after the slaves were "freed." As a society, we are still in the healing process from this oppression and its results.

Cultural and social rage is an explosive release from the depths of suppressed emotion. This is just like the rage we have explored in this book, resulting from childhood abuse and abandonment. It is empowered by the years of pain, fear and anger resulting from oppression. It brings about destruction and bloodshed, but it also brings necessary change. We have seen this not only in the rage against racism, but in the responses of early feminists in their rage against sex discrimination. Adolescence can be viewed as a (sometimes violent) process of breaking free from the "oppression" of childhood. As long as there is oppression, there will be suppression and explosions of rage. It is inevitable. Solving the problems leading to oppression is what a large part of the world's population is about. What we are about in this book is giving rise to healthy empowerment within individuals to minimize suppression and oppression as much as possible.

Long-term constructive change, both personal and societal, comes from the healthy use of anger for effective transformation of oppressive systems. This is now being accomplished by many individuals who use appropriate and yet powerful means to bring about fair and equitable treatment of all people. To me, this is healthy expression of anger.

Many of us are angry at the abuse of this planet, our home. The best way to channel this emotional energy is to put it into hard work for creating a healthy, safe planet. To attack violently those we feel have abused our environment simply causes new problems which distract us from the task at hand. I am not against political and social activism. As a matter of fact I actively support some environmental protection and conservation groups. I am only aware that we all cannot and do not need to become political and social activists to help with the restoring of our planet to good health. Recycling, for example, gives each of us an opportunity to take individual responsibility and put our emotional energy into immediate constructive action.

There are always constructive means for positive action. If you are in a situation in which you feel victimized and powerless, find that blank spot in your mind where the solution to your problem is supposed to be and isn't. Now just be still with that silence and emptiness, in the absence of your answer. Learn to be comfortable not knowing, and you will know all you need to know when you need to know it. The answer will gradually appear in the blank space, or the problem will work itself out. Many times our problems are primarily a result of our emotional reactions to situations. When we become still and silent, we often find the problem vanishes like a cloud on a windy day.

A SPECIES IN RECOVERY

One way of looking at the human situation is to see us as a species in recovery. We are recovering from a wide variety of small-minded, short-sighted, naive views of the world and our place within it. Following are some of those mistakes in thinking from which it is my belief we are in recovery:

- We thought we were better and more important than non-human life forms. We saw ourselves as superior and therefore devalued and abused the plant and animal kingdom. We are indeed glorious beings. Our greatest sin is self-negation and failure to use the magnificent gifts we were given. When we begin to see ourselves as better than other life forms, however, we have lost sight of reality. We are totally dependent on this planet and all of its life forms for our physical existence. All of the life forms on this planet are mysterious and wonderful, and they deserve respect whatever our relationship to them may be.

- As a result of the belief that we are better than other life forms, we have struggled to develop power over them. This has led to great destruction and grief. We are like an ignorant, untamed being who is given a beautiful home filled with magnificent possessions. In this analogy, the untamed being systematically destroys all of his possessions. Through our own ignorance, we destroy and neglect our gifts until they are worthless. We are in recovery from just that same type of ignorance, in terms of how we have treated the earth and its life forms.

- We thought that some of us human beings were better than others. We have neglected, abused, robbed and killed our fellow human beings. We have unleashed blind, ignorant rage among ourselves and suffered greatly for it. Our wars have been helpless reactions to fear and oppression. We have divided up our planet into sections and attacked each other across the lines.

  This is just one small planet. We are all sticking off the sides of it, held into the center by a force we call gravity. We are each equally powerful and equally insignificant. Our existence is the result of a fragile, delicate balance the likes of which we have not found anywhere else in the universe. We have to learn to live together, now. It is time. We are all the same in the ways that really matter, and each of us deserves to live as much as the other.

- We thought our sexuality was bad, and both genders have as a result rejected the other in a subconscious attempt to avoid being led astray. We have managed to get ourselves totally confused where gender and sexual relations are concerned. Sexual abuse, sex addiction, sexism and the dissolution of the family are some of the devastating results of this confusion.

  Our sexuality is as natural and beautiful as the flowers and the sunshine. The differences between the genders add to the mystery and the wonder of life and relationship. The act of making love is a sacred communion between two people which is ideally a physical, emotional and spiritual union. When we begin to realize these and other similar truths, tremendous healing will occur.

- We have confused touching with sex and aggression. We have virtually stopped touching each other, except in one of these two ways. Many people go through their entire lives deprived of nurturing, loving touch. We must find new, safe ways of touching each other in order to survive as a species.

    Fred Donaldson, Ph.D., is a pioneer in the field of teaching and expanding upon a unique form of touch. He has written several articles on his work with children and wild animals, focusing on an innovative form of play which involves what appears to be a universal language of touch. Of all the work done in this area, Dr. Donaldson's stands out as truly addressing the need for non-aggressive, non-competitive and non-sexual touch.

- We forgot how to play. Because of the sharp edges of competition and aggression, most of us stopped playing early in our childhood. We got too serious too soon. As a psychotherapist focusing on the healing of the inner child, I am acutely aware of the need for play as a part of the recovery process. The lighthearted, carefree attitude of play is one we need, not only as children, but throughout our lives. Again I refer to Dr. Fred Donaldson as an authority on play. If I were to say this to him, he would immediately defer to the children and animals who have been his playmates and teachers. Information on Dr. Donaldson's work (play) can be obtained by contacting Renaissance Educational Associates, 4817 North County Road 29, Loveland, Colorado 80538-9515, 303-679-4309.

- We thought our emotions were only something that needed controlling. We even thought some of our feelings were just plain bad. Correcting this misunderstanding has been a primary focus of this book.

- We thought this life was merely a testing ground to see if we qualified for the next one, which was to be either heaven or hell. Because of this, we have lived for many years in guilt and fear, believing people are basically sinful. This has been the cause of great suffering, and it has caused us to devalue the miracle of existence. Recovery means to begin to realize the heaven that is here now. We must also take responsibility for healing the bits of hell we have created here on earth.

As we claim our worth and value as physical, intellectual, emotional and spiritual beings, we are recovering from these and many other related mistakes in our thinking. Before we can recognize that this planet is our home and that all other species of life are members of our family, we must come home within our own skins. We cannot deny our physical bodies and embrace the planet with love. Taking care of and loving the environment starts with taking care of and loving ourselves. Each of us is the center of our own universe. When we love ourselves, we are loving the world.

This body is my home.
This planet is my home.
I am at home in my body.
I accept and embrace all that I am.
My commitment to myself and to the world is to
value and care for this gift of life that I am.

APPENDIX

AFFIRMATIONS EXERCISE

I. Physical

  A. Target areas
    1. Exercise
    2. Diet
    3. Health maintenance

  B. New thought/affirmation

    1. I, _____ release the need for/to

    (second and third person for writing exercise, for example, "You, Bill release . . ." and "He, Bill releases . . .")

    _____

    2. I, _____ deserve _____

    _____

    3. I, _____ am experiencing _____

    _____

    4. Negative or contradictory thoughts which arose

    were _____

    _____

5. Affirmations to replace these negative thoughts are _____

II. Mental

A. Target areas
   1. Openness (to open my mind)
   2. Authority (to claim the authority of my mind over my actions)
   3. Knowledge and consciousness expansion

B. New thought/affirmation

   1. I, _____ release the need for/to

   _____

   _____

   2. I, _____ deserve _____

   _____

   3. I, _____ am experiencing _____

   _____

   4. Negative or contradictory thoughts which arose were _____

   _____

   5. Affirmations to replace these negative thoughts are _____

   _____

III. Emotional

A. Target areas
   1. Experience (to give myself permission to experience my feelings)
   2. Expression (to openly express my emotions)
   3. Stability (to affirm emotional stability in my life)

B. New thought/affirmation

1. I, _____ release the need for/to

_____

_____

2. I, _____ deserve _____

_____

3. I, _____ am experiencing _____

_____

4. Negative or contradictory thoughts which arose
were _____

_____

5. Affirmations to replace these negative thoughts
are _____

_____

IV. Relationships

A. Target areas
  1. Boundaries (to affirm my right to clear, flexible boundaries)
  2. Intimacy (to give myself permission to be intimate)
  3. Openness (to create open communiation in my relationships)

B. New thought/affirmation
  1. I, _____ release the need for/to

_____

_____

  2. I, _____ deserve _____

_____

  3. I, _____ am experiencing _____

_____

  4. Negative or contradictory thoughts which arose
  were _____

_____

5. Affirmations to replace these negative thoughts
are _____

_____

V. Financial

A. Target areas
   1. Opportunity (to open my mind to new financial possibilities)
   2. Planning
   3. Managing

B. New thought/affirmation
   1. I, _____ release the need for/to

   _____

   _____

   2. I, _____ deserve _____
   _____

   3. I, _____ am experiencing _____
   _____

   4. Negative or contradictory thoughts which arose
   were _____

   _____

   5. Affirmations to replace these negative thoughts
   are _____

   _____

VI. Professional

A. Target areas
   1. Knowledge
   2. Skills
   3. Development

B. New thought/affirmation
   1. I, _____ release the need for/to

_____

_____

2. I, _____ deserve _____

_____

3. I, _____ am experiencing _____

_____

4. Negative or contradictory thoughts which arose
were _____

_____

5. Affirmations to replace these negative thoughts
are _____

_____

REFERENCES

Bly, Robert, **Iron John,** Addison Wesley, 1990.

Bradshaw, John, **Healing The Shame That Binds You,** Health Communications, 1988.

Bradshaw, John, **Homecoming: Reclaiming and Championing Your Inner Child,** Bantam, 1990.

Exeter, Michael, **Living At The Heart Of Creation,** Foundation House Publications, 1990.

Fishel, Ruth, **The Journey Within: A Spiritual Path To Recovery,** Health Communications, 1987.

Hay, Louise, **You Can Heal Your Life,** Hay House, 1987.

Pearsall, Paul, **Superimmunity,** McGraw-Hill, 1987.

Sullivan, H.S., **The Interpersonal Theory of Psychiatry,** Norton Publishing, 1953.

Whitfield, Charles, **A Gift To Myself,** Health Communications, 1989.

AUDIOCASSETTES

For healthy anger management and expression:

Anger: Deal With It Before It Deals With You, 4-tape album, Bill DeFoore, Ph.D. Music soundtrack by Steven Halpern, 1988. $39.95 + $2.50 S/H.

Helping Your Children With Anger: A Guide For Parents, 2-tape album, Bill DeFoore, Ph.D., 1991. $19.95 + $2.00 S/H.

For affirmation and self-nurturing:

Nurturing Your Inner Child, Bill DeFoore, Ph.D. Music soundtrack by Steven Halpern, 1989. $10.50 + $2.00 S/H.

Affirmations For Well Being, Bill DeFoore, Ph.D. Music soundtrack by Steven Halpern, 1988. $10.50 + $2.00 S/H.

For overcoming compulsive and addictive disorders:

Smoking Cessation, Bill DeFoore, Ph.D. Music soundtrack by Steven Halpern, 1988. $10.50 + $2.00 S/H.

Compulsive Eating: You Can't Quit Until You Know What's Eating You! 6-tape album with workbook, Donna LeBlanc, M.Ed. Music soundtrack on tapes 9, 10, 11, and 12 by Steven Halpern, 1989. $59.95 + $2.50 S/H. 2-tape album, $19.95 + $2.00 S/H, 1989, Donna LeBlanc, M.Ed.

For more information regarding tapes and programs offered at the Institute for Personal and Professional Development, Inc., write to I.P.P.D., Inc., 4201 Wingren, Suite 201, Irving, TX 75062. 800-322-4773. To order tapes, make checks payable to New Tape Enterprises, 4201 Wingren, Suite 201, Irving, TX. 75062. Texas residents include 8.25% sales tax.